FOR
REFERENCE ONLY

-01/11

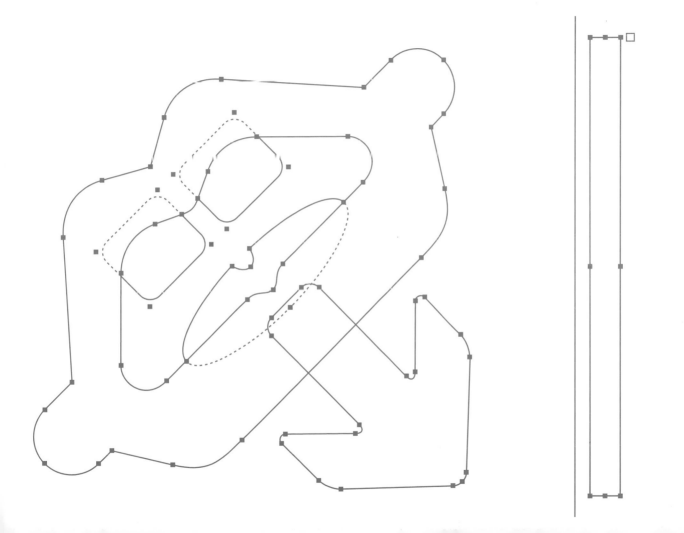

lingua grafica

Edited by Robert Klanten
Concept: MUTABOR (Johannes Plass, Heinrich Paravicini)
Written by Johannes Plass, Carsten Raffel
Layout and Design by Carsten Raffel, Monika Hoinkis
Additional Productions: Heike Herrmann, Steffi Lohmann

Die Deutsche Bibliothek-CIP-Einheitsaufnahme
Lingua Grafica
Hrsg. von Robert Klanten, Hendrik Hellige, Michael Mischler. Berlin: Die Gestalten Verlag, 2001
ISBN 3-931126-59-5

For your local dgv distributor please check out: www.die-gestalten.de

MUTABOR lingua grafica ➜ Major reference work for image language – Die Gestalten Verlag, Berlin

This book belongs to:

_____

_____

_____

_____

_____

 MUTABOR lingua grafica
Major reference work for **image language** – Die Gestalten Verlag

0001–1360

All of the symbols were developed and clicked by the Mutabor designers:

Anna Bertermann, Julia Bünger, Simone Campe, Axel Domke, Stefan Ecks, Silke Eggers, Mareile Hanke, Monika Hoinkis, Jessica Hoppe, Minka Kudrass, Stefanie Lohmann, Paul Neulinger, Frederik Niclaus, Lars Niebuhr, Heinrich Paravicini, Christoph Petersen, Elisabeth Plass, Johannes Plass, Carsten Raffel, Till Raubacher, Stefanie Tomasek, Behruz Tschaitschan, Julica Vieth (†)

➜

➜

Thank you:

Ever since the first rough sketches were drawn, characters and symbols have been influenced by the symbol tool, the clip-on area and the visual theme as a real object or a visual concept.

The characters in this book were created on the Mac with **Macromedia**'s highly-rated #TP tool **Freehand** (from Version 3.1 to the current Version 9.0), and influenced by digitally-recorded rough sketches and their lines together with all the potential of the tools in the programme.

This book is dedicated, in a spirit of deep gratitude, to everyone who contributed to the development of this wonderful programme, including all of its endearing quirks and non-functions.

MUTABOR

 You are here.

002/003 004/005 006/007 008/009 010/011 012/013 014/015 016/017 018/019 020/021 022/023 024/025

026/027 028/029 030/031 032/033 034/035 036/037 038/039 040/041 042/043 044/045 046/047 048/049

050/051 052/053 054/055 056/057 058/059 060/061 062/063 064/065 066/067 068/069 070/071 072/073

074/075 076/077 078/079 080/081 082/083 084/085 086/087 088/089 090/091 092/093 094/095 096/097

098/099 100/101 102/103 104/105 106/107 108/109 110/111 112/113 114/115 116/117 118/119 120/121

122/123 124/125 126/127 128/129 130/131 132/133 134/135 136/137 138/139 140/141 142/143 144/145

146/147 148/149 150/151 152/153 154/155 156/157 158/159 160/161 162/163 164/165 166/167 168/169

170/171 172/173 174/175 176/177 178/179 180/181 182/183 184/185 186/187 188/189 190/191

I

5

10

PRAEFATIO ⇨

Argumento argumentis non egente liber iste signa visualia vel symbola notasque imaginum (icones) tractans praefationem verbosam minime requirit. Tum symbola tum notae imaginum quasi litterarum formae sunt universae societatis. Ab infinito tempore eiusmodi signa ibi sunt in usu ubi homines diversarum linguarum communicare solent.

 Symbola litteris certe antecedunt historialiter scilicet homo depinxit gallinam ovumque (vel ovum gallinamque) priusquam ea litteris mandare didicit.
　　Symbola notasque imaginum ex deductionabilibus et investigabilibus artibus sive speciebus visualibus computoque cognoscimus que praecipue per saeculum praeteritum ad studium pertinuerunt picturae linearis et adhuc pertinent. His temporibus signa varia et multiforma magno numero diffusa adhibentur ubicumque nuntiis quanta maxima potest celeritate communicare oportet.

In hoc libro non divulgare intendimus historiam integram symbolorum quod abunde ab aliis alibi factum est. *Lingua Grafica* liber noster primus ex MUTABOR editus patefacere debeat multiplicitatem signorum excogitatorum cusorumque annis MCMXCV ad MM tam manu singuli pictoris quam ex philosophia et principio domus nostrae: MUTABOR.

➜ Mutabor!

15

20

25

30

Qualitates bonorum symbolorum scilicet notio, gradus abstractionis, solutio ficta sequuntur → ▭ Pars 1
leges bonae picturae. Notione nata graduque abstractionis ex locatione symboli futuri considerato
tandem solutio secundum *formam, imaginem, cogitationem* fingitur.

In prima parte libri nostri selectio parva symbolorum signorumque convenientium postula-
tionibuseximiis praescriptis offertur.

Secunda pars praecepta dabit lectorem atque vias probatas ostendet ad perveniendum ad operam → ▭ Pars 2
perfectam.

In tertia vel ultima parte amplissima collectio numerata symbolorum signorumque optimorum → ▦ Pars 3
in domo nostra ortorum atque ex inexhaustibilibus archivis nostris quaesitorum indice exornata
invenitur. Sic *Linguam Graficam* instrumentum necessarium atque utilissimum omni designatori
picturae linearis cito fieri in dubio non est. ⇐ AUCTORES

I

5

PREFACE ⇨

A book on the subject of visual symbols, icons and logos does not need a long preface. The 10
contents of this book are self-explanatory. Icons and logos are the characters of the global society.
Signs like these have been used for as long as anyone can remember wherever people with different
mother tongues need to register and comprehend information quickly and concisely.

Seen historically, the visual symbol certainly preceded the character. Before he could write, the 15
human being would have drawn, say, a chicken and an egg (or egg and chicken) to communicate
the subject to his opposite number.

Icons and logos are well known from road signs, scientific orientation systems, phenotypes
and the whole EDP field. They have become a part of our general knowledge, and on the creative
side they have been an integral element of the training of graphic designers for a century. 20

These signs have been caught up in an inflationary spiral since the emergence of screen design:
Desktop interfaces, mobile data carriers and of course the Internet have produced a veritable
flood of icons. They are used wherever a pictorial symbol can impart the desired information
more quickly than a combination of characters.

25

But this book is not intended to be a lecture on the history of the icon — other authors have
already dealt with that subject more than adequately. With *Lingua Grafica*, MUTABOR's first published
book, we document the multitude of icons that came into being during the last few years of our
work, from 1995 to 2000. They were shaped not only by the hand of the individual designer, but
➜ Mutabor!   also by the design philosophy and general maxim of the company: »I will change«. 30

The quality which people expect from a hard-hitting symbol is well known. The most important factors are the idea, the degree of abstraction, the formal solution and — crucially — the linking of these three aspects.

Once the idea has been born, the degree of abstraction required is dependent on the environment in which the symbol will appear. The formal solution is subject to the basic rules of drawing, which can be consulted in any textbook under the headings *illustration, presentation* and *image*. Individuality and uniqueness are imparted by the hand of the designer, and are often influenced by the fashionable currents in graphic design.

The first part of this book presents a small selection of icons and logos which fulfil the requirements in a most exemplary fashion — as can be verified in their application. The grand opening will follow this preface. ➜ ☐ Part 1

Unfortunately, the criteria for a good icon are observed only infrequently — and taught even more rarely. Formal brilliance is rare, with bad copies of well-known, strong symbols or effects from the DTP toolkit being the general, regrettable rule. For this reason, we want to use the second part of this book to provide an insight into our workshop and show readers some ways of creating the perfect icon. ➜ ☐ Part 2

In the third, final and most voluminous part we provide a list of the 1360 best logos, icons and word-and-picture symbols that have been created within our company. It took weeks of diligent work to fish them out of the inexhaustible MUTABOR archives, sort them and give each of them an identification number. The index at the end of this volume provides a coherent overview — on every conceivable subject — of the occasionally highly diverse pictorial interpretations of the designers. In this way *Lingua Grafica* should quickly become an indispensable, inspirational tool for every designer. ⇐ THE AUTHORS ➜ ▦ Part 3

VORWORT ⇨

Ein Buch mit der Thematik visuelle Zeichen, Bildsymbole (Icons) und Bildmarken benötigt kein langes Vorwort. Die Inhalte dieses Buches sind selbsterklärend. Icons und Bildmarken sind die Schriftzeichen der globalen Gesellschaft. Wann immer Menschen unterschiedlicher Sprachen Informationen schnell und prägnant erfassen und verstehen müssen, werden solche Zeichen seit Ewigkeiten verwendet.

Wagt man den historischen Rückblick, so stand das Bildsymbol sicherlich vor dem Schriftzeichen. Bevor er zu schreiben lernte, zeichnete der Mensch Henne und Ei (oder Ei und Henne), um seinem Gegenüber dieses Thema zu vermitteln.

Aus Wegeleit- und wissenschaftlichen Orientierungssystemen, Erscheinungsbildern und dem EDV-Bereich sind Icons und Bildmarken bekannt und Teil des Allgemeinwissens geworden, in der Kreation sind sie seit einem Jahrhundert Bestandteil der Ausbildung zum Grafikdesigner.

Inflationär sind diese Zeichen seit den Anfängen der Screen-Gestaltung: Desktop-Oberflächen, mobile Datenträger und natürlich das Internet haben geradezu eine Icon-Flut produziert. Überall dort, wo Bildsymbole eine Information schneller als eine Kombination aus Schriftzeichen vermitteln können, werden sie verwendet.

In diesem Buch wollen wir jedoch nicht über die Geschichte des Bildsymbols referieren, dieses wurde bereits von anderen Autoren umfassend geleistet. Mit *Lingua Grafica*, MUTABORs erster Buchpublikation, dokumentieren wir die zahlreichen Bildsymbole, die während unserer Arbeit in den vergangenen Jahren von 1995 bis 2000 entstanden sind. Sie wurden von der Handschrift des einzelnen Designers ebenso geprägt wie von der Designphilosophie und Lebensmaxime des Hauses: »Ich werde mich verwandeln.«

➜ Mutabor!

Die Qualitätsanforderungen an ein prägnantes Zeichen sind bekannt. Es geht in erster Linie um die Idee, den Abstraktionsgrad, die formale Lösung und vor allem um eine sinnvolle Verknüpfung dieser drei Aspekte.

Ist die Idee geboren, so ist der Abstraktionsgrad abhängig von dem Umfeld, in dem das Zeichen steht. Für die formale Lösung gelten die Grundregeln des Zeichnens, die sich in jedem Lehrbuch unter den Begriffen *Abbildung, Darstellung* und *Vorstellung* nachschlagen lassen. Individualität und Einzigartigkeit entstehen unter dem Duktus des Designers und unterliegen nicht selten den modischen Strömungen des Grafikdesigns.

Der erste Teil dieses Buches präsentiert eine kleine Auswahl von Icons und Bildmarken, die diese Anforderungen aufs Vorbildlichste erfüllen, wie sich in der Anwendung nachprüfen lässt. Die Vernissage gleich nach diesem Vorwort.

➜ Teil 1

Für ein gutes Bildsymbol gelten Kriterien, die leider zu selten beachtet und noch seltener gelehrt werden. Formale Brillanz ist selten, schlechte Kopien von bekannten und starken Zeichen oder Effekte aus der DTP-Kiste sind leider die Regel. Deshalb wollen wir in dem zweiten Teil dieses Buches einen kleinen Einblick in unsere Werkstatt gewähren und dem Leser mögliche Wege zum perfekten Icon aufzeigen.

➜ Teil 2

Im dritten, abschließenden und raumgreifendsten Teil findet sich schließlich eine Auflistung der 1360 besten im Hause entstandenen Logos, Icons und Wortbildmarken, in wochenlanger Fleißarbeit aus den schier unerschöpflichen Archiven von MUTABOR gefischt, sortiert und mit einer Kennnummer versehen. Im Index am Ende dieses Bandes lassen sich nun zu jedem beliebigen Thema die bisweilen sehr unterschiedlichen Bild-Interpretationen der Designer nachvollziehen – auf diese Weise sollte *Lingua Grafica* schnell zu einem unverzichtbaren Inspirationswerkzeug für jeden Gestalter werden. ⇐ DIE AUTOREN

➜ Teil 3

1

PREFACE ⇨

5

Un ouvrage consacré à la thématique des signes visuels, symboles graphiques (icones) et marques figuratives se passe aisément d'une longue préface. C'est le cas de celui-ci: les contenus parlent d'eux-mêmes. Icones et marques figuratives sont les types de caractères qu'utilise la société planétaire. De tels symboles existent depuis la nuit des temps; ils interviennent chaque fois que des individus de langues différentes doivent comprendre et enregistrer des informations 10 rapidement et durablement.

Historiquement parlant, il est certain que le symbole graphique a précédé le caractère. Avant d'apprendre à écrire, l'homme a dessiné la poule et l'œuf (ou l'œuf et la poule) pour communiquer ce sujet à son entourage.

15

Panneaux de signalisation routière, systèmes d'orientation scientifiques, logos, domaine de l'informatique: les icones et marques figuratives nous sont devenues familières et font désormais partie des connaissances générales ; dans le domaine créatif, elles sont intégrées à la formation de designer graphique depuis un siècle.

C'est avec l'utilisation de l'écran comme interface que ces symboles vont connaître une véritable 20 inflation: les bureaux électroniques et supports de données mobiles, sans oublier Internet, bien entendu, ont généré une multitude d'icones. Partout où les symboles graphiques sont en mesure de transmettre une information plus vite que ne le ferait une combinaison de caractères, ils sont systématiquement utilisés.

25

Notre propos n'est cependant pas de retracer l'historique du symbole graphique, ce qui a déjà été fait de façon exhaustive par d'autres auteurs. Avec *Lingua Grafica* (première publication d'ouvrage de MUTABOR), nous avons voulu présenter les nombreuses icones qui ont vu le jour de 1995 à 2000 dans le cadre de notre travail. Elles portent la signature de leur auteur tout en traduisant

➜ Mutabor! la philosophie de design ainsi que la maxime de la maison: »Je me transforme«.

30

Les exigences de qualité auxquelles tout symbole prégnant se doit de satisfaire sont connues. Il s'agit en premier lieu de l'idée, du degré d'abstraction, de la solution formelle et, avant tout, de la combinaison de ces trois aspects.

Une fois que l'idée est née, le degré d'abstraction dépend de l'environnement dans lequel se situe le symbole. La solution formelle est soumise aux règles fondamentales du dessin, énoncées dans tous les manuels aux chapitres *Illustration*, *Représentation* et *Présentation*. L'individualité et l'unicité naissent sous la plume du designer et obéissent généralement aux tendances du moment en matière de design graphique.

La première partie de cet ouvrage présente une petite sélection d'icones et de symboles graphiques satisfaisant à ces exigences de façon exemplaire, comme on peut le vérifier dans l'application. Le vernissage suit immédiatement cette préface.

→ Partie 1

Une bonne icone obéit à des critères qui, regrettablement, sont trop rarement respectés et encore plus rarement enseignés. La virtuosité formelle demeure l'exception, tandis que les mauvaises copies de symboles prégnants ou les effets issus de la PAO sont malheureusement monnaie courante. C'est pourquoi, dans la seconde partie de notre ouvrage, nous ouvrons au lecteur les portes de notre atelier et lui présentons diverses méthodes pour parvenir à l'icone parfaite.

→ Partie 2

Dans la troisième et dernière partie, qui est aussi la plus importante, se trouve une liste des 1.360 meilleurs logos, icones et marques nominatives/figuratives créés dans notre maison. En un long et minutieux travail, ils ont été sélectionnés parmi les archives MUTABOR — source quasiment inépuisable —, classés, puis pourvus d'un numéro d'identification. L'index qui figure à la fin de l'ouvrage permet, à partir d'un thème quelconque, de découvrir les interprétations graphiques — parfois très différentes — de chacun des créateurs, ce qui devrait rapidement faire de *Lingua Grafica* un outil d'inspiration indispensable à tout designer. ⇐ LES AUTEURS

→ Partie 3

I

PROLOGO ⇨

5

Un libro dedicado a la temática de signos visuales, símbolos iconográficos (iconos) y marcas no precisa un prólogo amplio. Los contenidos de este libro se entienden y explican por sí mismos. Iconos y marcas de imagen son los signos de la sociedad global. Este tipo de signos ha sido utilizado desde siempre, allí donde personas de diferentes procedencias y diferentes idiomas 10 deben comprender y entender de forma rápida y precisa la información recibida.

Al hacer una retrospectiva histórica, podemos constatar que el símbolo iconográfico aparece antes que los signos de escritura. Antes de aprender a escribir, el hombre dibujó la gallina y el huevo (o el huevo y la gallina) para comunicarse sobre este tema con sus vecinos. 15

En los sistemas de orientación y señalización direccional científicos, las señales y el sector de la informática, los iconos y las marcas de imagen son conocidos y se han convertido en parte de los conocimientos generales. En la creación son, desde hace un siglo, parte integrante de la formación de los diseñadores gráficos.

Estos signos proliferan desde los comienzos de la creación en pantalla: superficies para 20 escritorios, soportes de datos portátiles y móviles, y naturalmente, Internet, han producido una verdadera avalancha de iconos. Los símbolos iconográficos son utilizados allí donde pueden transmitir una determinada información de modo más rápido que una combinación de signos alfabéticos.

25

En este libro no queremos hacer una historia de los símbolos iconográficos, esto ya ha sido realizado ampliamente por otros autores. Con *Lingua Grafica* (Lenguaje gráfico), el primer libro publicado por MUTABOR, documentamos los numerosos símbolos creados entre 1995 y 2000. Se distinguen tanto por el estilo propio del diseñador como por la filosofía de diseño y lema de la casa: »Me transformaré«.

➜ Mutabor!

30

Las exigencias de calidad de un signo gráfico exacto y conciso son bien conocidas. Se trata en primer lugar de la idea, del grado de abstracción, la solución formal y, sobre todo, de la combinación de estos tres aspectos.

Una vez surgida la idea, el grado de abstracción depende del campo para el que se crea el signo. Para la solución formal se utilizan las reglas fundamentales del signo, que pueden encontrarse en cualquier manual bajo los conceptos *reproducción, representación* y *concepto*. El carácter único e individual es creado por el diseñador y está sujeto con frecuencia a las corrientes de moda del diseño gráfico.

La primera parte de este libro presenta una breve selección de iconos, símbolos y marcas que cumplen estos requisitos a la perfección, tal y como puede comprobarse en la aplicación. La exposición se muestra tras este prólogo.

➜ Parte 1

Para crear un buen símbolo iconográfico deben seguirse una serie de criterios que desafortunadamente pocas veces se tienen en cuenta y, aún en menos ocasiones, se enseñan. La brillantez formal escasea, las malas copias de signos conocidos y los efectos del repertorio DTP son por desgracia demasiado frecuentes. Por esta razón, en la segunda parte de este libro queremos hacer un pequeño resumen de nuestro taller y mostrar al lector posibles caminos para crear un icono perfecto.

➜ Parte 2

En la tercera parte, concluyente y la más amplia, presentamos una recopilación de los 1.360 mejores logotipos, iconos y marcas de imagen con palabras creados en la empresa, rescatados en semanas de arduo trabajo de los archivos casi inagotables de MUTABOR, seleccionados y clasificados con un número. En el índice al final de este volumen se retoman en todos los temas las, en ocasiones, muy diferentes interpretaciones de la imagen dadas por los diseñadores; de este modo, *Lingua Grafica* se convertirá rápidamente en una fuente de inspiración indispensable para todos los diseñadores. ⇦ LOS AUTORES

➜ Parte 3

序 ⇨

視覚に訴える記号、図形シンボル（アイコン）、シンボルマーク等をテーマとする本書は自ずとその内容を語るものであり、長々しい序文は必要としません。アイコンやシンボルマークはグローバル社会の文字といえます。しかし夫々異なる言語を使う人々が、情報を素早く、また簡明的確に把握・理解する必要があるところには、昔から記号やシンボルが使われてきました。

歴史を振り返ると、記号やシンボルは既に文字が発明される前から使用されていました。まだ文字を持たなかった人類の祖先は、例えば雌鳥と卵（または卵と雌鳥）を描くことによって、それを相手に伝えようとしました。

交通標識や学問上で使われる多くの記号、表象や電子データ処理分野のアイコンやシンボルマークは今ではごく一般的で、既に一般教養として浸透しています。また創造の分野においては 100 年来、グラフィックデザイナーの必須課目となっています。

これらの記号やシンボルは、スクリーン・デザインの始まりとともに、とりわけ頻繁に使用されるようになってきました。デスクトップや携帯電話、それにインターネットがアイコンの氾濫を導き、今ではそれを使用することによって文字よりも早い情報交換が可能な全ての部分に使用されています。

記号やシンボルについて書かれた書物は数多く、本書はそれを目的とするものではありません。『リンガ・グラフィカ』はムタボール（MUTABOR）社が初めて手掛ける出版物で、ここには 1995 から 2000 年に考案されたシンボルマークの数々が収集されています。個々のシンボルは考案者の個性で彩られ、同時に私どものデザイン哲学と生活の金言ともいえる『私は変身する』の表現でもあります。

➔ Mutabor!

1

5

10

15

20

25

30

記号やシンボルには常に簡明的確性が要求されます。そこではまず構想を抽象化し、それに形（フォルム）を与えるという作業、つまり構想と抽象化と造形の統合に重点がおかれます。

まずアイディアが生まれ、次にそれが抽象化されますが、その際シンボルの使用される環境が重要な条件となります。デザインにおいては、どの教科書にも出ている『模写、描写、表現の原則』が当てはまります。

独創性は個々のデザイナーの作風であり、往々にしてグラフィック・デザインの流行の影響下にあります。

本書第 I 章には、要求されるデザイン性と高機能性を備えたアイコンやシンボルマークの最優秀作品を集めています。序文に続いてこれらの作品が紹介されています。　→ ▭ 第1章

通常、一体何をして優れたシンボルマークとするのかという基準には余り関心が払われず、またデザイナーにはそれを学ぶ機会も極めて少ないというのが現状です。その上、優れたデザイン性を持つものも少なく、よく目にするマークや強烈な印象を受けるシンボル、または DTP のデザインの模倣が往々にして行われています。このような理由から、第 2 章では、ムタボール社でアイコンが出来上がる迄の全作業工程を紹介しています。　→ ▭ 第2章

最後の第 3 章では最大のページ数を割いて、私どもが作成したロゴ、アイコン、シンボルマークの中から特に優れた I360 件を選出、紹介しています。これらはムタボール社の膨大な資料の中から何週間もかけて厳選・整理し、番号付けしたものです。後ろの索引には時として全く予期しないようなデザイナー自身によるシンボルの解釈が添えられています。最後に本書『リンガ・グラフィカ』が、グラッフィク・デザイナーのインスピレーションを刺激する上で必要不可欠のツールとなることを祈ってやみません。⇐ 発行者　→ ▦ 第3章

30

(one)

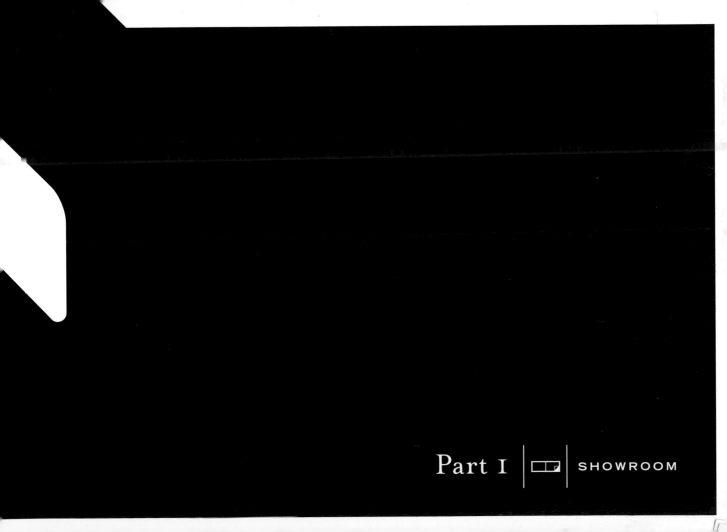

Part I | SHOWROOM

Mutabor IIII, CD 1.) Communication 2.) Corporate design 3.) Changes of course

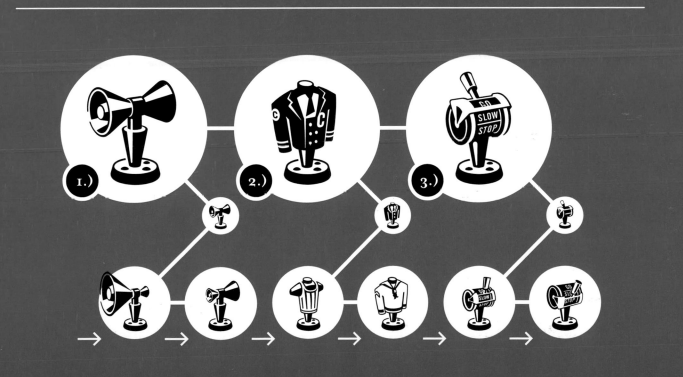

Menzel Nolte Heinemann, Feuerwasser + Brandlöscher: Icons for 2 drink cans

cola

Höchststand 0.33 Ltr.

cola

NACH DEM GEBRAUCH SOFORT WIEDER AUFFÜLLEN!

DANGER

Nur bei brennendem Durst trinken!

040 / 39 82 10

EXPLOSIVE

Menzel Nolte Heinemann

BRANDLÖSCHER©

BRANDLÖSCHER©

C

C

Schweiz

0.33 ltr.

printed by printCan GmbH. CH · 8207 Schaffhausen

Mindestens haltbar bis: siehe Bodenprägung

cola getränk Zusammensetzung: Coffeinhaltige Limonade, Wasser, Zucker, Kohlensäure, Cola-Limonadengrundstoff (mit Farbstoff Zuckercouleur, Zitronensäure, Aci-Phosphorsäure), natürliche Säurungsmittel Phosphorsäure), Coffein-Aroma.

limo

kühl lagern!

Voll seetüchtig!

100%
wiederauffüllbar

Sorgt für einen kühlen Kopf!

040 / 39 82 10

Gehört in jedes Rettungsset.

Menzel Nolte Heinemann

limo

FEUERWASSER©

FEUERWASSER©

W

M

Schweiz

0.33 ltr.

printed by printCan GmbH. CH · 8200 Schaffhausen

Mindestens haltbar bis: siehe Bodenprägung

limo getränk Fruchtsaft Limonade mit 4% Fruchtsaft. Zusammensetzung: Wasser, Zucker, Orangensaft, Kohlensäure, Säurungsmittel, Zitronensäure, Mandarinensaft, Zitronensaft, natürliche Fruchtaromen, Antioxidans, Ascorbinsäure, Farbstoff Beta Carotin.

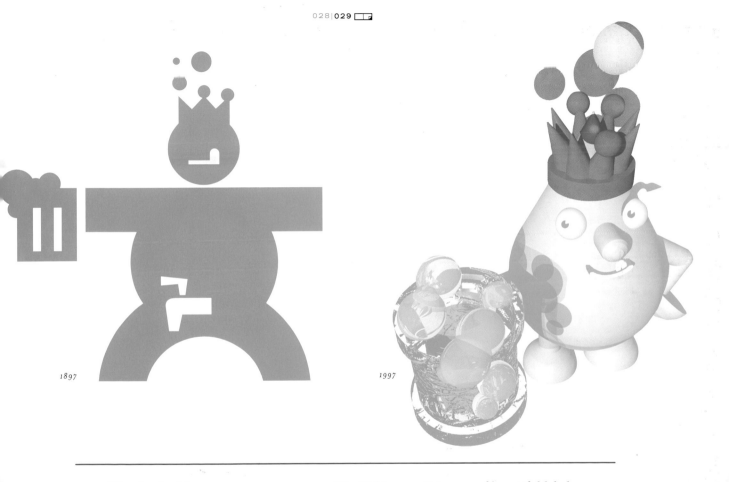

1897

1997

Mutabor's oldest customer, 100 years of Pax Vobiscum, 100 years of beautiful labels

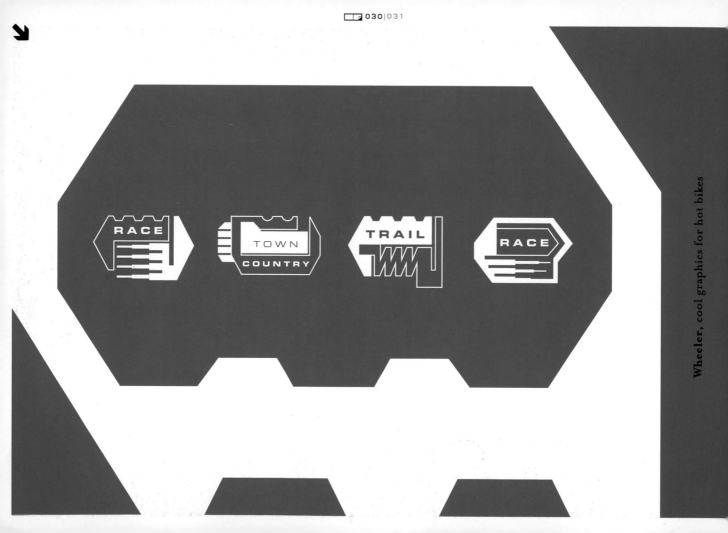

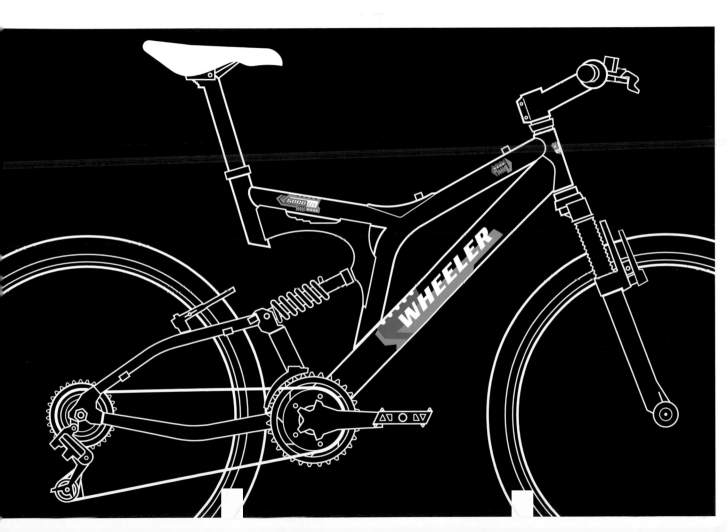

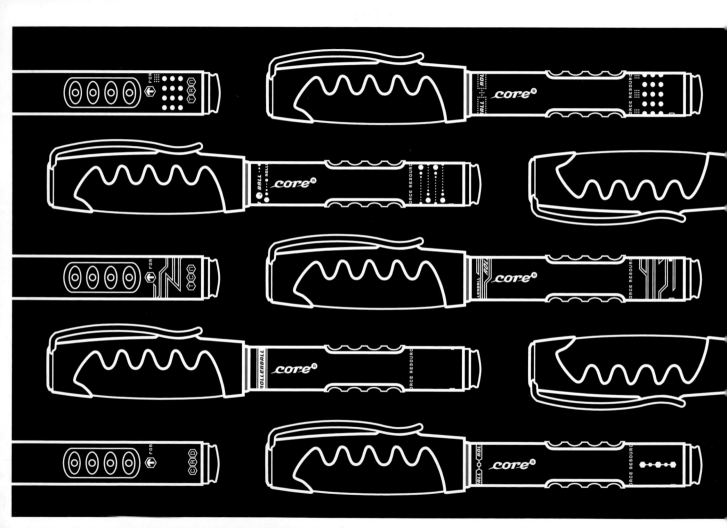

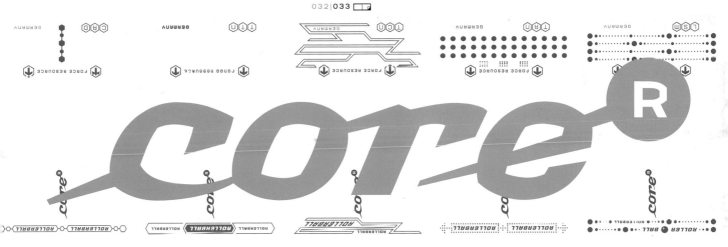

Rotring Core, graphics for fountain pens and rollerballs

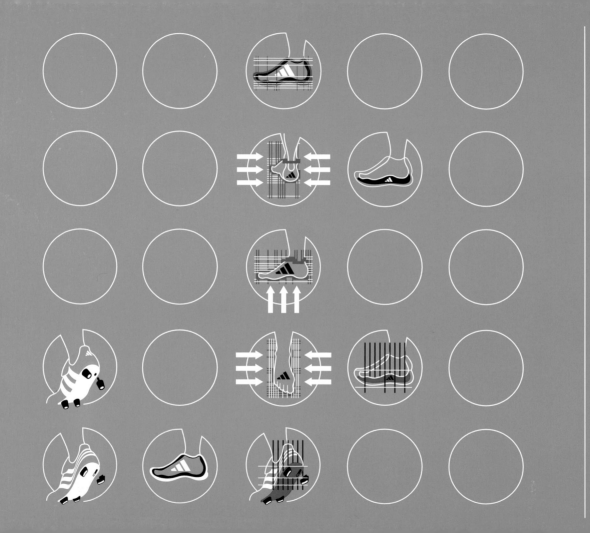

adidas, icons for shoeboxes and other packaging

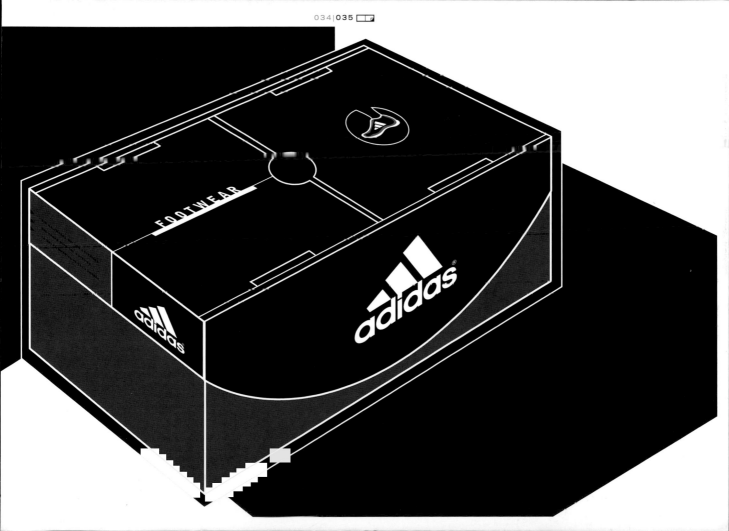

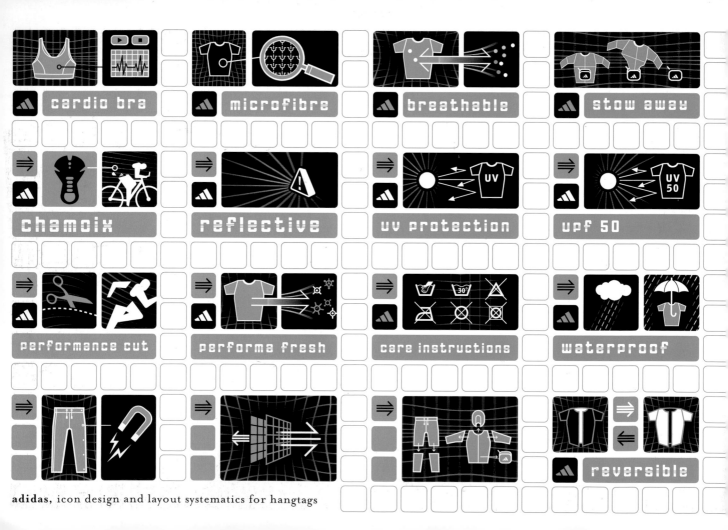

cardio bra

microfibre

breathable

stow away

chamoix

reflective

uv protection

upf 50

performance cut

performa fresh

care instructions

waterproof

reversible

adidas, icon design and layout systematics for hangtags

Nastrovje Potsdam, icons for men's outer clothing

(before)

(after)

CoreMedia AG, corporate identity from A to Z

MEDIACORE

keyboard layouts, special

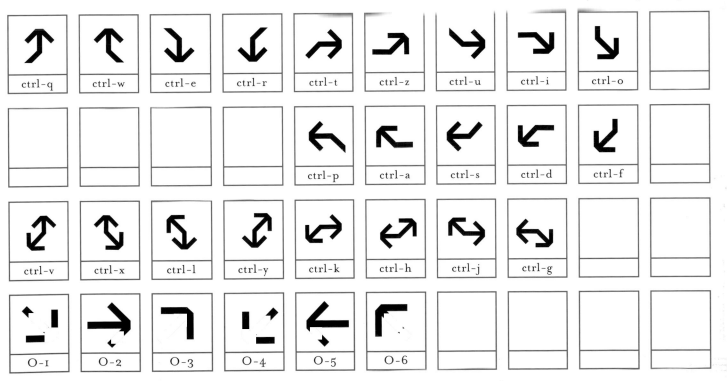

ctrl-q	ctrl-w	ctrl-e	ctrl-r	ctrl-t	ctrl-z	ctrl-u	ctrl-i	ctrl-o
				ctrl-p	ctrl-a	ctrl-s	ctrl-d	ctrl-f
ctrl-v	ctrl-x	ctrl-l	ctrl-y	ctrl-k	ctrl-h	ctrl-j	ctrl-g	
O-1	O-2	O-3	O-4	O-5	O-6			

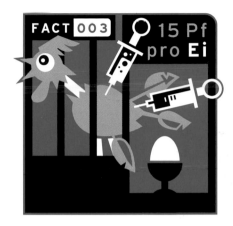

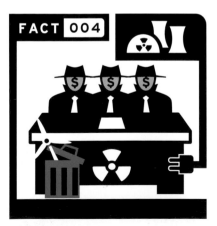

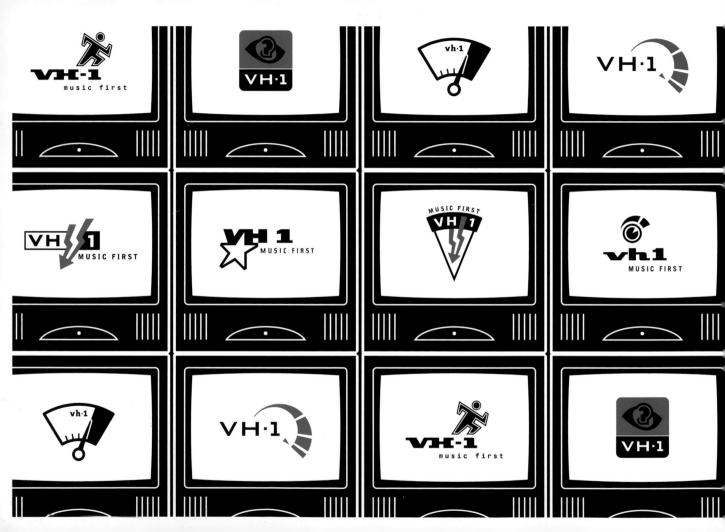

VH-1 Music First, network identity proposal

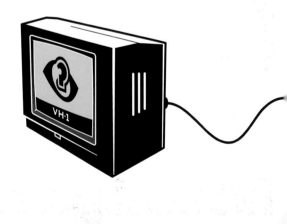

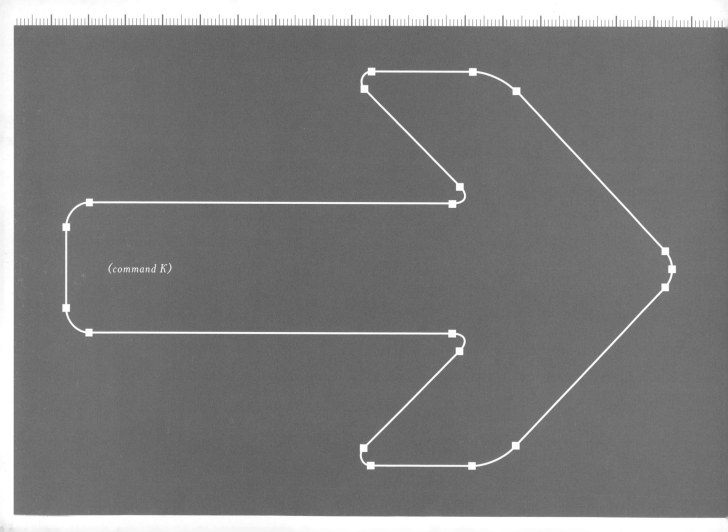

(command K)

Part 2 WORKSHOP

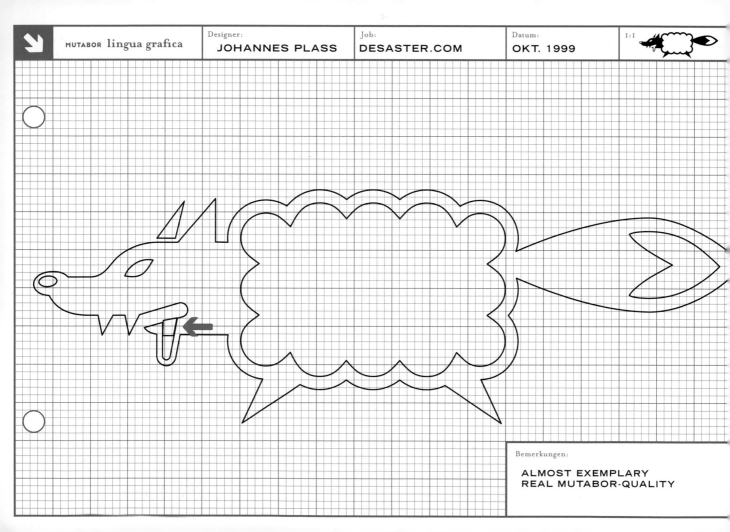

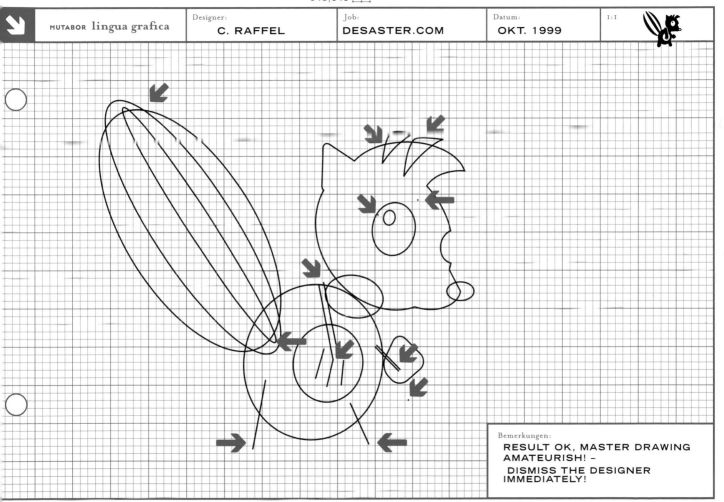

MUTABOR lingua grafica

Designer: C. RAFFEL

Job: DESASTER.COM

Datum: OKT. 1999

1:1

Bemerkungen: RESULT OK, MASTER DRAWING AMATEURISH! –
DISMISS THE DESIGNER IMMEDIATELY!

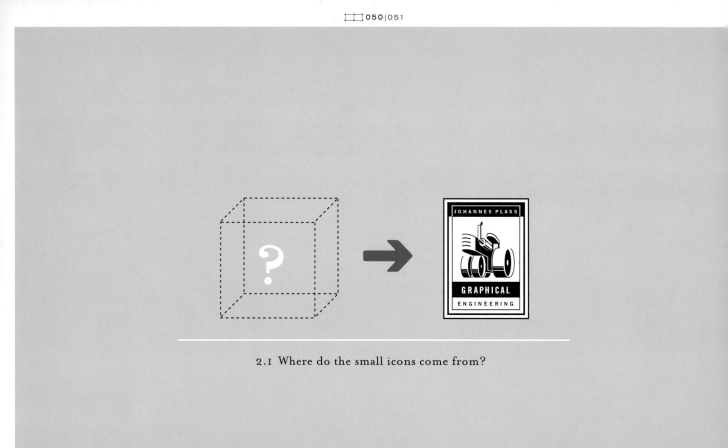

2.1 Where do the small icons come from?

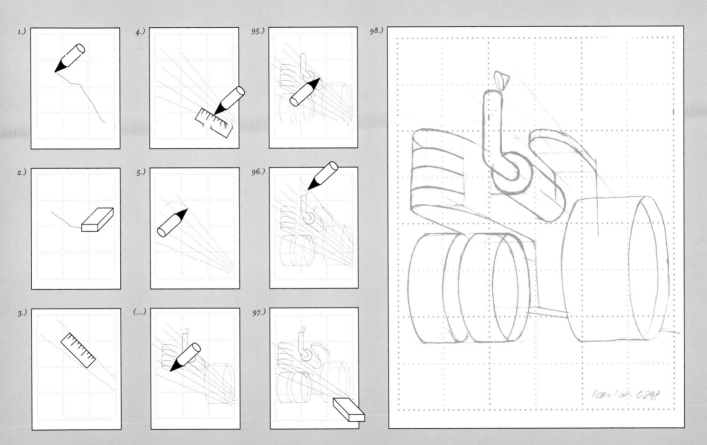

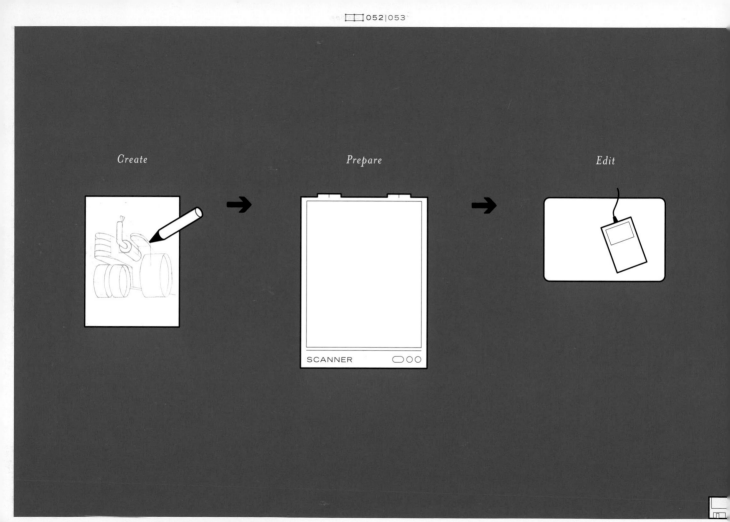

Create

Prepare

Edit

SCANNER

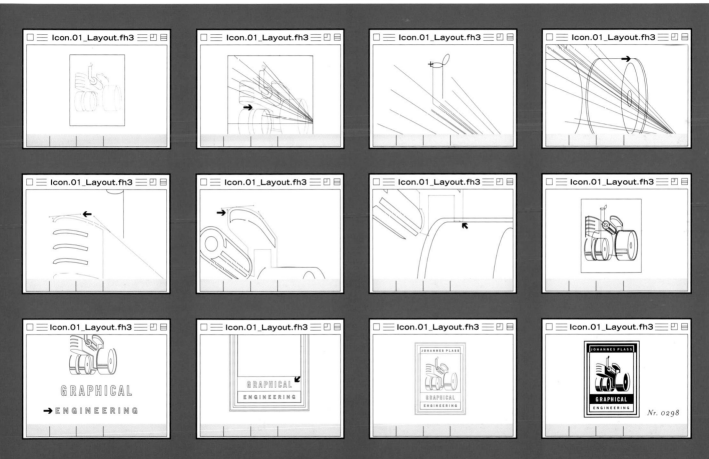

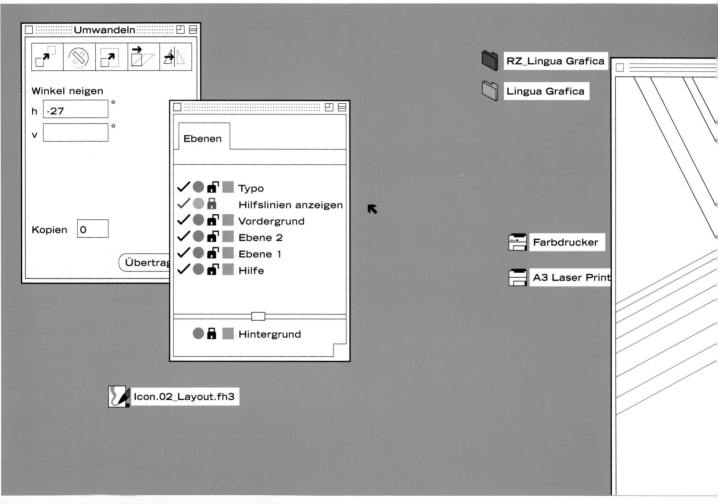

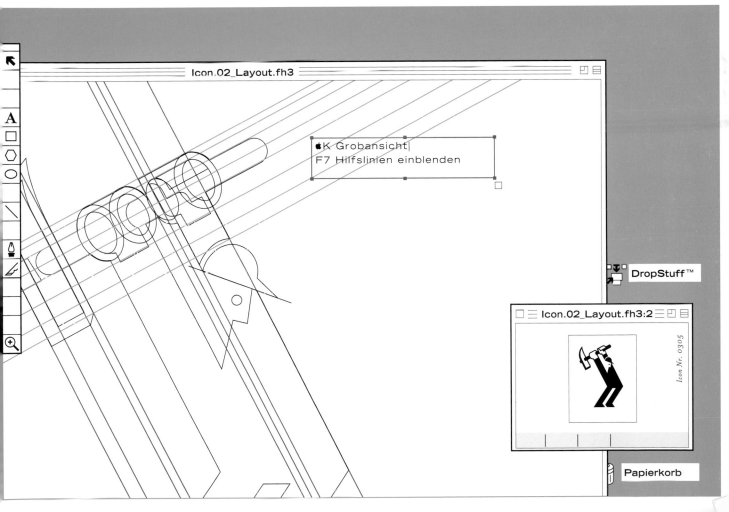

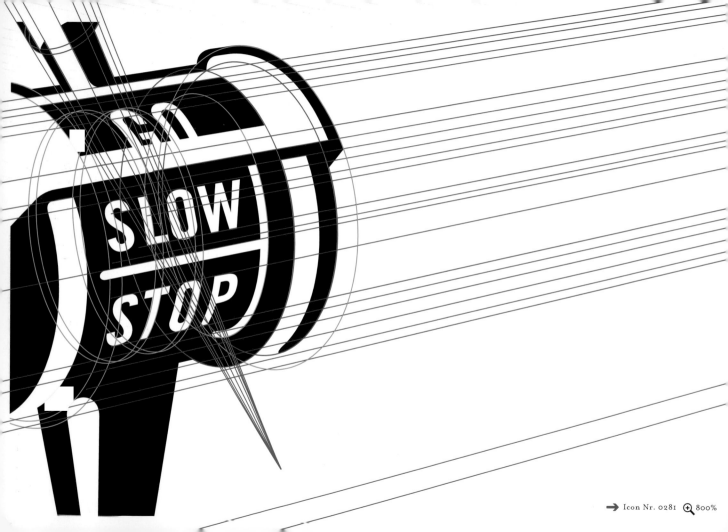

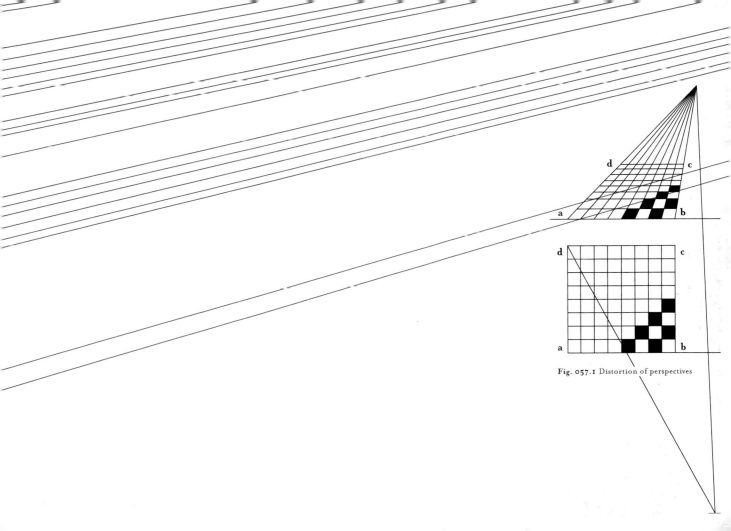

Fig. 057.1 Distortion of perspectives

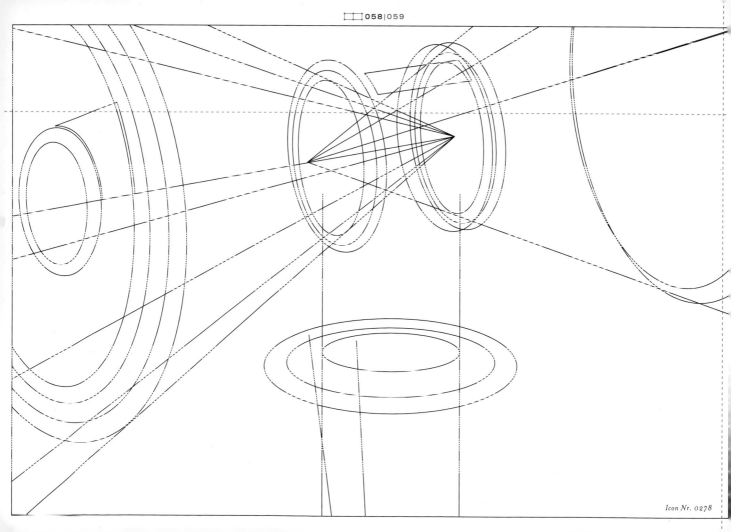

⌘N, ⌘R, ⌐⌘M, F7,
r, x=16,21; y=14,7;
h=150,00; h=145,00,
v, x=10; y=45,
F7, F7, F6, ⌘S,
r, e, p; x=5; y=7,
v, z, v,
e; h=10; b=45,
⌘0, ⌐⌘0, ⌘A,
F7, F12, F12,
v; x=-10,5;
y=158,254;
h=20; b=5, ⌘D, ⌘Z,
⌘Z, v, X=16; Y=8,
⌘Z, ⌘Y, ⌐⌘0, ⌘A,
⌘0, p, v, p, v, p, v, p,
v, p, v, p, v, p, v, p, v,
p, v, p, v, p,
F6, ⌘S, F7, F7, v,
r; X=32; Y=42,
e; h=35; b=36,
v, p, v, p, v, ⌘0, v, ⌘D,
⌘Z, v, ⌘D, ⌘Z, ⌘Y, z,

⌐⌘0, ⌘A, p, v, ⌘S,
F12, F12,
v; x=150; y=-5,
t, v, t,
⌘S, v, ⌘0, v, p, ⌘D,
⌘Z, ⌘Y, ⌐⌘0, ⌘S, F7,
F7, F6, z,
v; h=10,00; h=15,00,
v; h=10,00, h=25,00,
u; x=10,7452; y=2v;
h=5,03; b=18,00,
v; h=45,90; b=11,00,
v, ⌘A,
v; x=1,234; y=0,21,
t, ⌘0, ⌘Z, ⌘Z, ⌘Z, ⌘Y,
⌘Y, ⌐⌘0, ⌘A,
v; x=5; y=0,58, p, v,
p, v, ⌘S, F7, F7,
r; x=30; y=60, r; x=10;
y=34,6432, v,
e; x=-8901; y=-554;
h=31; b=60,
v, p, v, p, v, ⌘D, ⌘0,

v, F7, F7 , ⌘D, ⌘Z,
⌘Y, ⌘Z, ⌘Z, ⌘Y
p, v, p, v, p, v, p, ⌘Z,
v, p, v, p, v, p, v, p, v,
p, z, v, p, v, p, v, p, v,
p, v, p, v, p, v, p, v, p,
v, p, v, p, v, p, v, p, v,
p, v, p, v, p, v, p, v, p,
v, p, v, p, z, v, p, v, p,
v, p, v, p, v, p, v, p, v,
p, ⌘K, ⌘K, v, p, v, p,
v, p, v, p, v, p, v, p, v,
p, v, p, v, p, v, p, v, p,
v, p, z, v, p, v, p, v, p,
v, p, v, p, v, p, v, p, v,
p, v, p, v, ⌘Z, ⌘K, ⌘K,
p, v, p, v, p, v, p, v, p,
v, p, z, p, v, p, v, p, v,
p, v, p, v, p, v, p, v, p,
⌘K, ⌘K, v, p, v, p, ⌘Z,
⌘Z, ⌘Z, ⌘Z, ⌘Z, v, p,
v, p, v, p, v, p, v, p, v,
p, v, p, v, p, v, p, v, p,

v, p, v, p, z, p, v, p, v,
p, v, p, v, p, v, p, v, p,
v, p, v, p, v, p, v, p, v, z,
v, p, v, p, v, p, v, p, v,
v, p, v, p, v, p, v, p, v,
p, v, p, ⌘Z, ⌘Z, p, v,
p, v, p, v, p,
⌐⌘0, ⌘S!, z, ⌘R, p,
v, p, v, p, v, p, v, p, v,
p, v, p, v, p, v, p, v, p,
v, p, v, p, v, p, v, p, v,
⌘R, F7, F7, F6,
v; x=160,50, y=5,00,
r, h=10,00; b=0,6, v,
F7, F7, F6, ⌘A, P,
⌘K, ⌘K, F7,
v; x=10; y=45,
t, […], ⌘0,
z, v, ⌘S, ⌘Z, ⌘Z, ⌘Z,
⌘Y, ⌘Y,
r; h=5,1; b=5,34,
r; h=6,6; b=2,
⌘A, F7, F7, F6, t, v,

⌘D, ⌘Z, ⌘0,
F7, F7,
r; x=12; y=45,
e; h=2,5; b=3,5, ⌘Z,
r; x=10; y=11, ⌘U, z,
v, p, v, p, v, v, p, v, p,
v, p, v, p, v, p, v, z, p,
v, p, v, ⌘Z, ⌘Z, p, v,
p, v, p, v, p, v, p, z, p,
v, p, v, p, v, p, v, p, v,
p, v, p, v, p, v, p, v, p,
v, p, v, p, v, p, v, p, v,
p, v, p, v, p, v, p, v, p,
v, p, v, p, v, p, z, p, v,
p, v, p, v, p, v, p, v, p,
v, p, v, p, v, p, v, p, v,
p, v, p, v, p, v, p, v, p,
v, p, v, p, v, p, v, p, v,
p, v, p, v, p, v, p, v, p,
v, p, v, p, z, p, v, p, v,
p, v, p, v, p, v, p, v, p,
⌘K, ⌘K, ⌘D, ⌘Z, ⌘0,
⌐⌘0, ⌘S, ⌘W, ⌘Q___

Select

_the basic tool. Often used between two other tools, or whenever these are converted into the selecting tool when the command key is pressed. Intensity of use (IU): 15 %

Text

_of course, an excellent icon can get along fine without this tool. Nevertheless, it does good work in the production of word marks, IU: 5 %

Rectangle/polygon/ellipse

_everything on God's earth can be dissected into squares, circles and triangles. This knowledge was not only put to good use by the Cubists; the clever icon clicker also works with these three tools frequently, especially in the drafting phase. Overall, he uses them about 20 % of the time. The beautiful stars of the polygon tool and the hexagons for the honeycomb design à la Core are also welcome guests, cf. pages 32/33

Line/pencil

_the line tool is used less often (for quick horizontals and verticals), and the pencil more often whenever the basic geometrical framework has to be redrawn more exactly and in greater detail, and when corners have to be rounded off, etc. The professional bending of curves, however, requires daily practice and at least six months' experience. Former Illustrator users often despair. Intensity of use, despite everything: 10+15=25 %

Knife

_often used at the late stage of the icon design process, when everything has to be cleared up and superfluous parts have to be trimmed. IU: 5 %

Enlarging

_and reducing. Used almost as frequently as the basic select tool, shall we say: 10 %

Arranging

_top, right, bottom, left, vertical centering, horizontal centering: the inclusion of these six tools in the basic toolbar is strongly recommended. The arrangement of different objects and/or individual armature items is completed quickly and with absolute precision. Mistakes are avoided, and headstrong magnetic auxiliary lines, which often make life difficult for the clicker, must be deployed only when it is genuinely useful to do so or when the work is supposed to look important. Intensity of use, total: 10 %

Unit/separating/overlapping/opening

_the circumspect image symbol designer likes using unit and opening tools, and does so often. One object can be made out of several, which is mostly of use when different geometrical forms are to be merged into one far more amorphous form. The opening tool can be used to punch interesting holes in boring objects. The calculated use of these four functions makes a great deal of painstaking curve bending unnecessary and reduces the use of the pencil tool to the necessary minimum. Average: 10 %

2.2 Plea for the
freehand-generated icon

→ 2.2.1

Icon Nr. 1202

- [X] Reduction of differences in stroke widths
- [X] Standardisation of line attributes
- [X] Proportionality of lines to surface

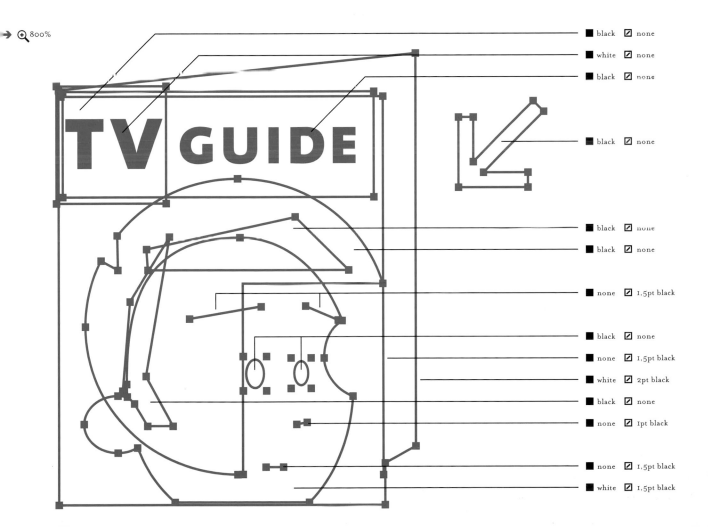

→ ⊕ 800%

■ black ☑ none
■ white ☑ none
■ black ☑ none

■ black ☑ none

■ black ☑ none
■ black ☑ none

■ none ☑ 1,5pt black

■ black ☑ none
■ none ☑ 1,5pt black
■ white ☑ 2pt black
■ black ☑ none
■ none ☑ 1pt black

■ none ☑ 1,5pt black
■ white ☑ 1,5pt black

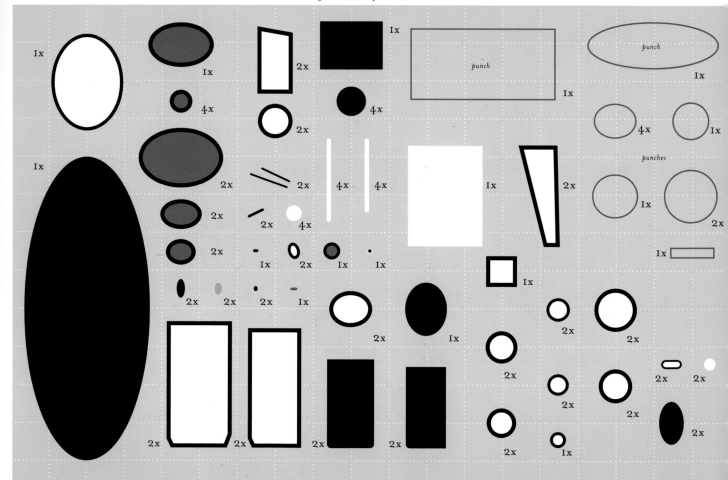

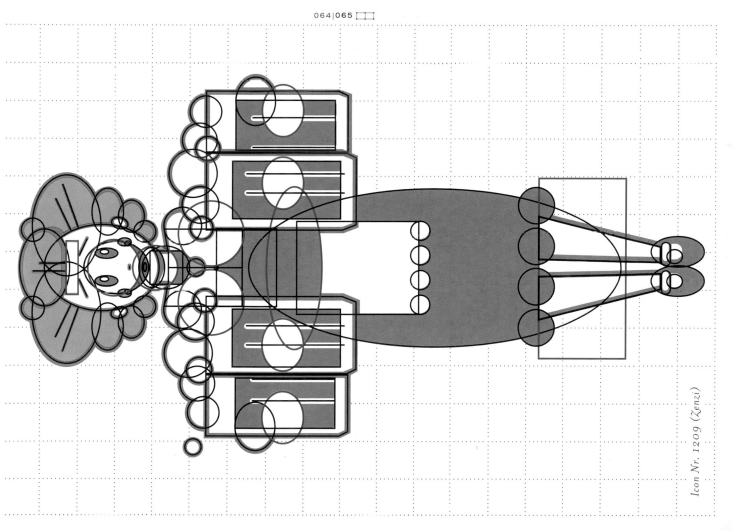

Icon Nr. 1209 (Zenzi)

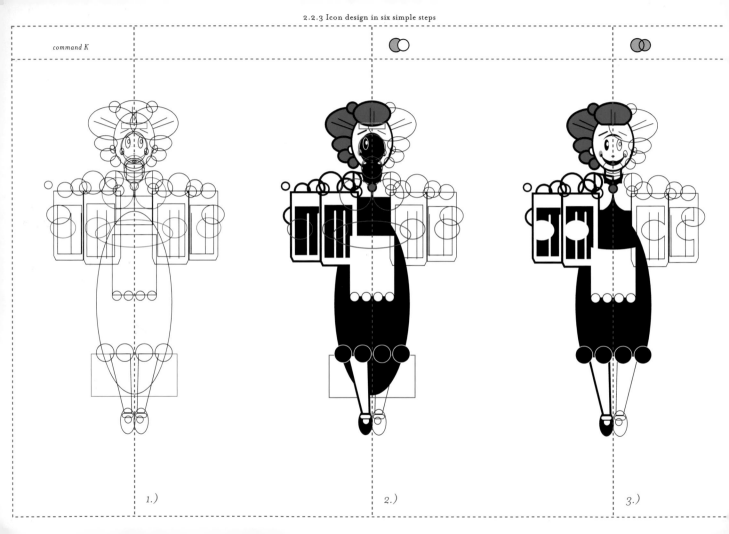

command K

1.)

2.)

3.)

duplication

finished!

4.)

5.)

6.)

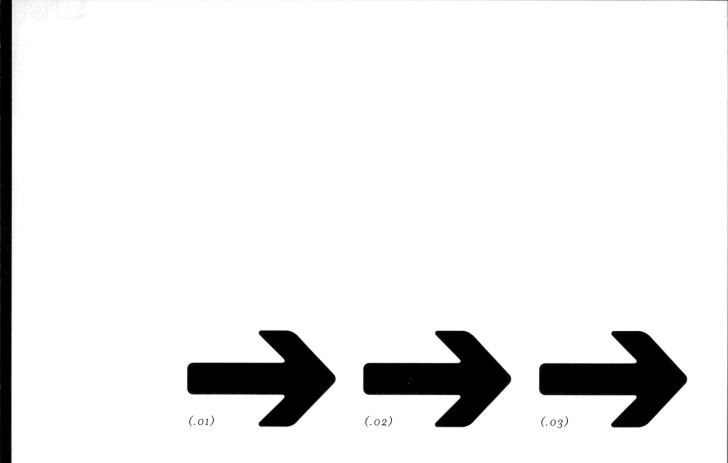

(.01)   (.02)   (.03)

Part 3 | STORAGE AND ARCHIVE

0001-0016 ➡

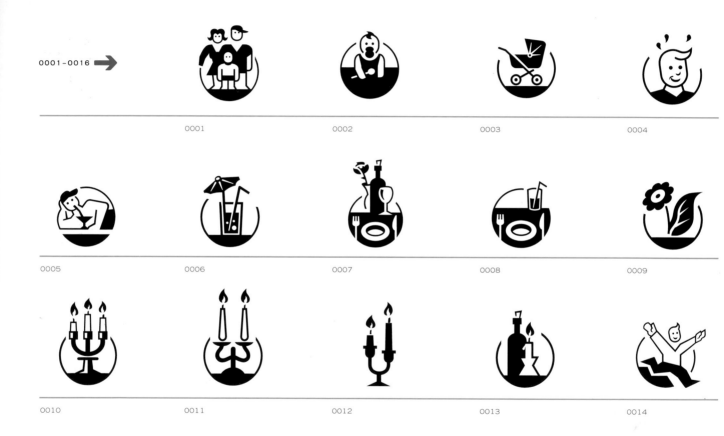

0001

0002

0003

0004

0005

0006

0007

0008

0009

0010

0011

0012

0013

0014

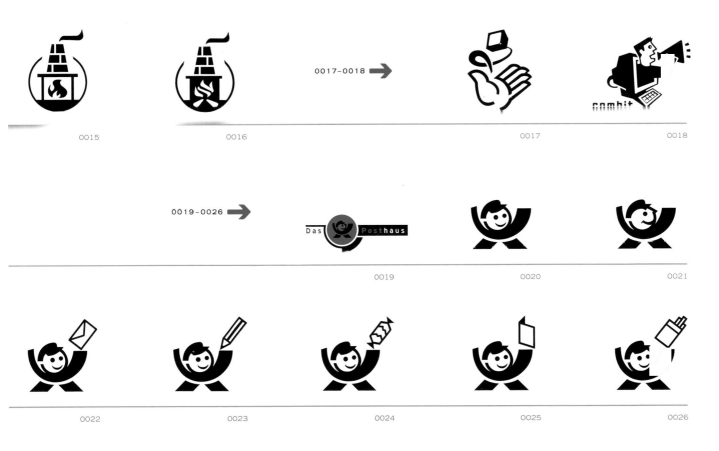

0015

0016

0017-0018

0017

0018

0019-0026

0019

0020

0021

0022

0023

0024

0025

0026

0015–0016 Adac Reisemagazin 0017–0018 Combit
0019–0026 Posthaus

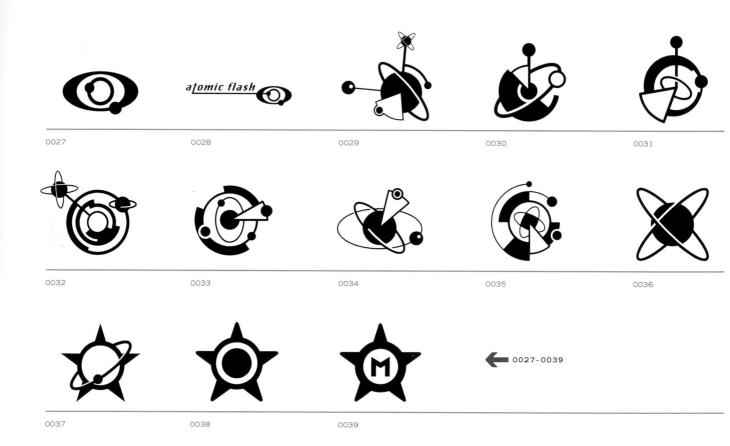

0027

0028 *atomic flash*

0029

0030

0031

0032

0033

0034

0035

0036

0037

0038

0039

⬅ 0027-0039

0040-0053 →

0040

0041

0042

0043

0044

0045

0046

0047

0048

0049

0050

0051

0052

0053

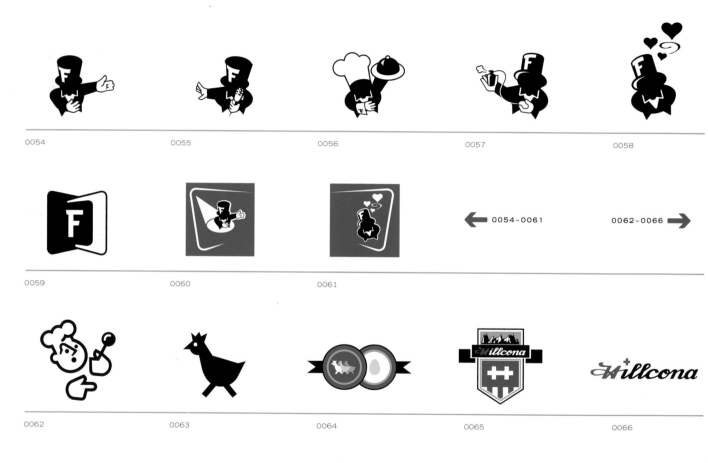

0054

0055

0056

0057

0058

0059

0060

0061

← 0054-0061

0062-0066 →

0062

0063

0064

0065

0066

0054–0061 Fortenbacher-Event
0062–0066 Hillcona

0067

0068

0069

0070

0071

0072

0073

0074

0075

0076

0077

0078

0079

0080

0081

0067—0081 Menzel Nolte

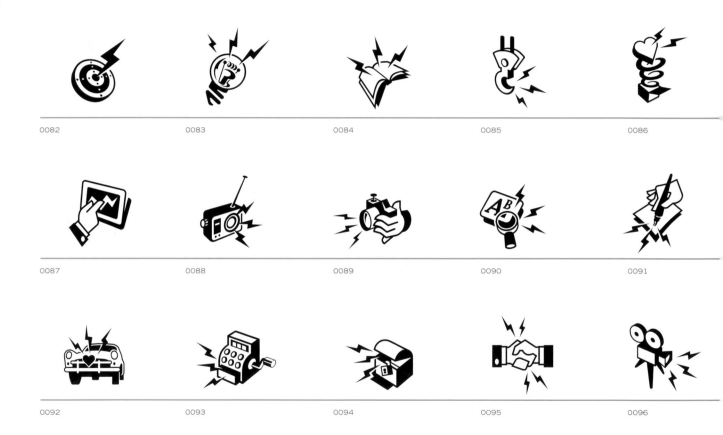

0082

0083

0084

0085

0086

0087

0088

0089

0090

0091

0092

0093

0094

0095

0096

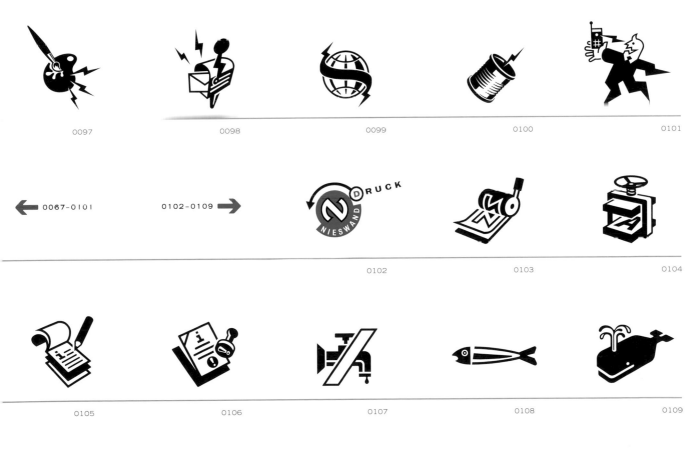

0097

0098

0099

0100

0101

◀ 0067–0101

0102–0109 ▶

0102

0103

0104

0105

0106

0107

0108

0109

0097–0101 Menzel Nolte
0102–0109 Nieswand Druck

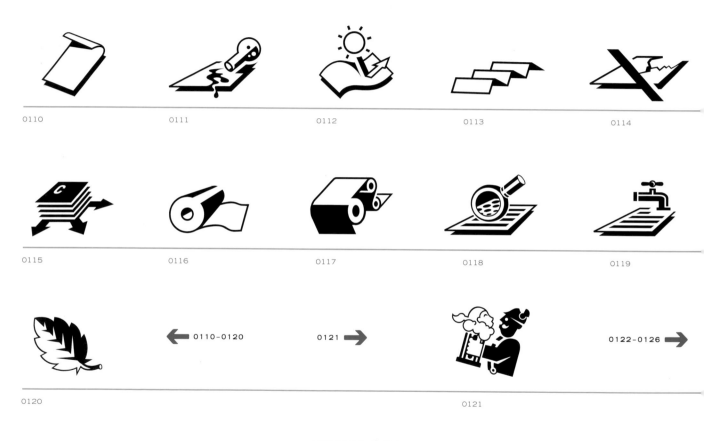

0110

0111

0112

0113

0114

0115

0116

0117

0118

0119

0120

← 0110–0120

0121 →

0122–0126 →

0121

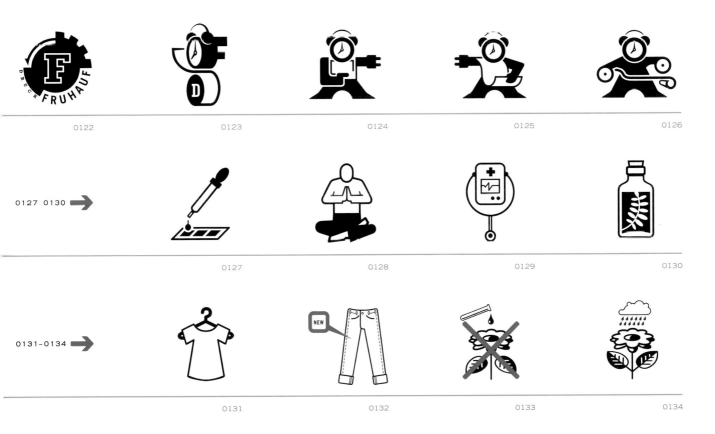

0122

0123

0124

0125

0126

0127 0130 →

0127

0128

0129

0130

0131–0134 →

0131

0132

0133

0134

0122–0126 Druckerei Fruhauf
0127–0130 Medicatum **0131–0134** Patagonia

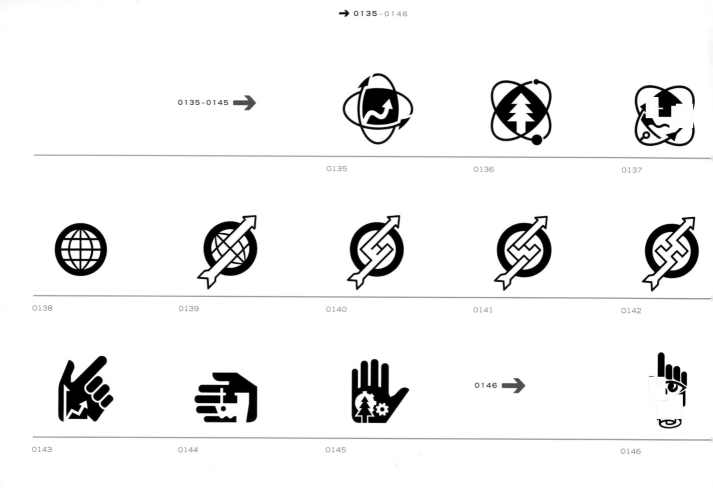

0135–0145 →

0135

0136

0137

0138

0139

0140

0141

0142

0143

0144

0145

0146 →

0146

0147-0224

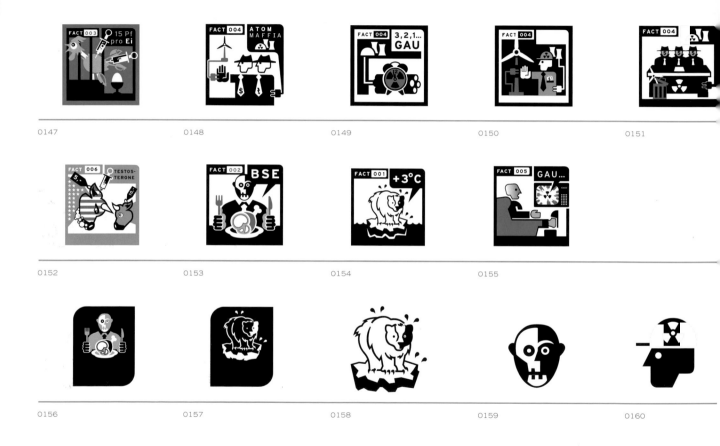

0147

0148

0149

0150

0151

0152

0153

0154

0155

0156

0157

0158

0159

0160

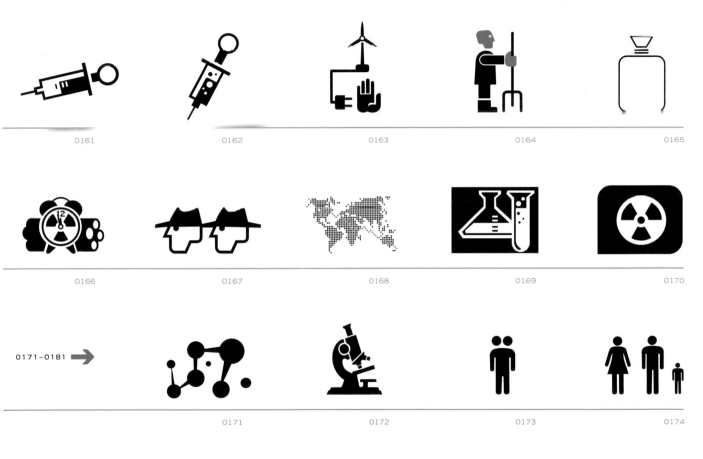

0161

0162

0163

0164

0165

0166

0167

0168

0169

0170

0171–0181 ➡

0171

0172

0173

0174

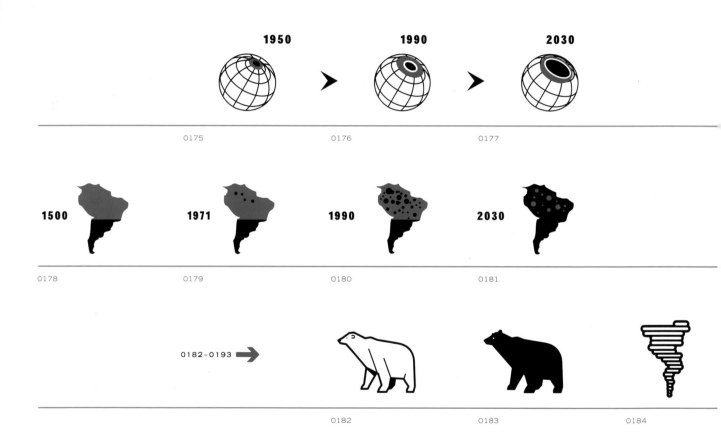

1950   1990   2030

0175   0176   0177

1500   1971   1990   2030

0178   0179   0180   0181

0182−0193 →

0182   0183   0184

0175−0181 Greenpeace
0182−0184 Greenpeace Magazin

0185

0186

0187

0188

0189

0190

0191

0192

0193

0194-0197 ➡

0194

0195

0196

0197

0185–0193 Greenpeace Magazin
0194–0197 Kids for Kids

0198

0199

0200

0201

0202

0203

0204

0205

0206

0207

0208

0209

0210

0211

0212

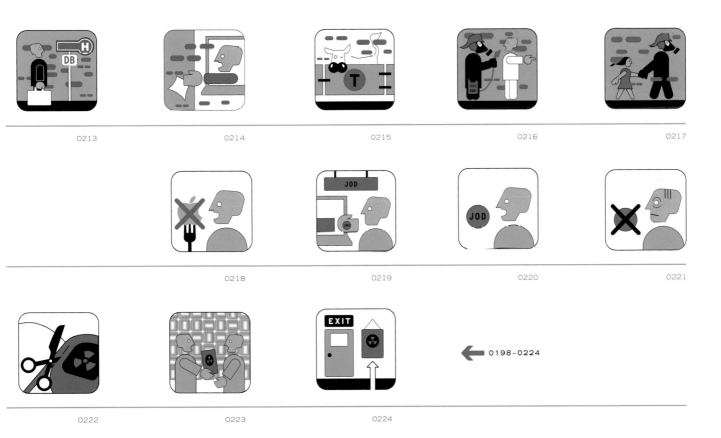

0213

0214

0215

0216

0217

0218

0219

0220

0221

0222

0223

0224

← 0198-0224

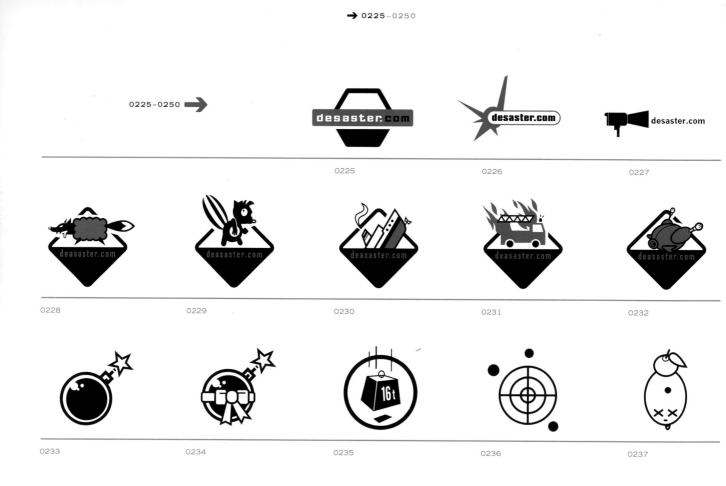

0225-0250 →

0225

0226

0227

0228

0229

0230

0231

0232

0233

0234

0235

0236

0237

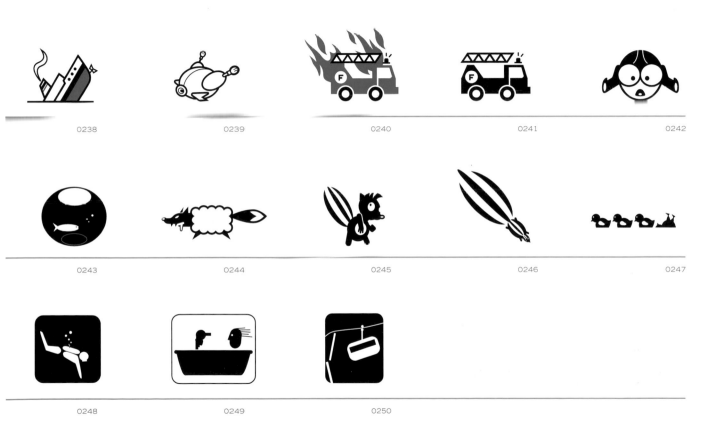

0238

0239

0240

0241

0242

0243

0244

0245

0246

0247

0248

0249

0250

0251-0270 →

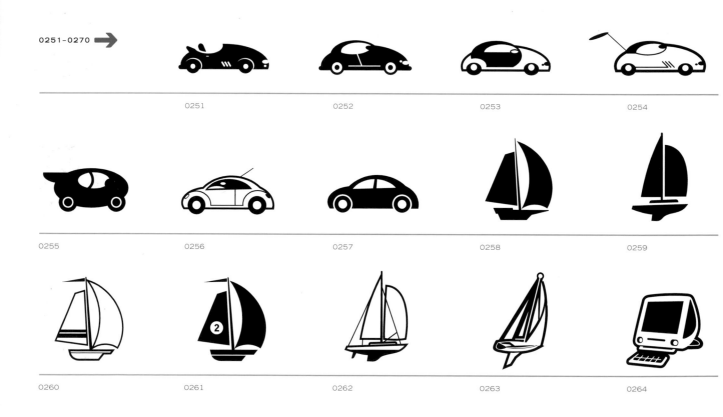

0251

0252

0253

0254

0255

0256

0257

0258

0259

0260

0261

0262

0263

0264

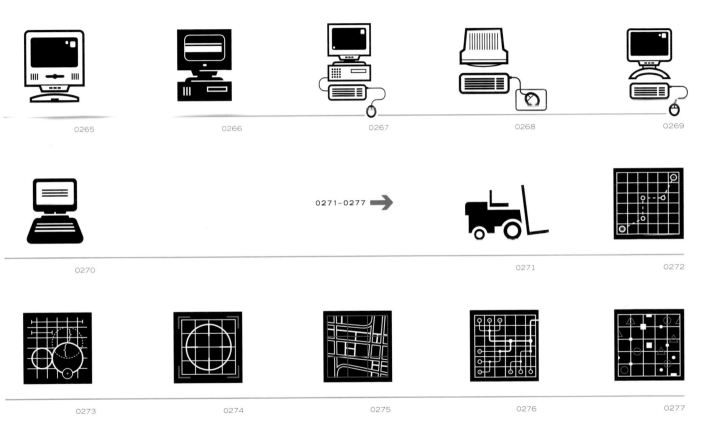

0265

0266

0267

0268

0269

0270

0271-0277 ➤

0271

0272

0273

0274

0275

0276

0277

0265—0270 Die Welt
0271—0277 Navigon Geometrics

➡ Mutabor Design, Barnerstrasse 63/Hof, 22765 Hamburg, Germany

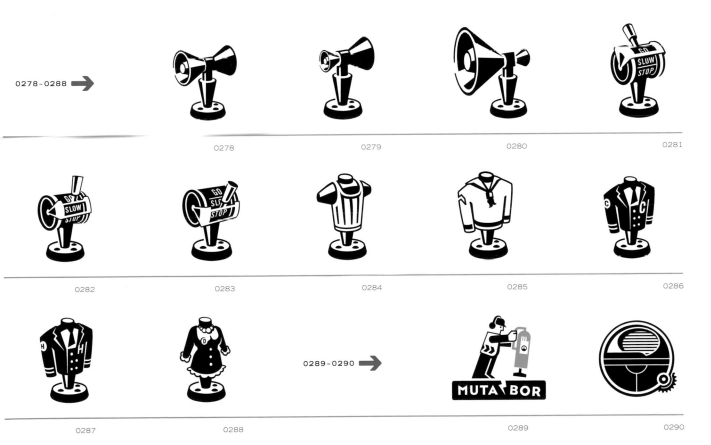

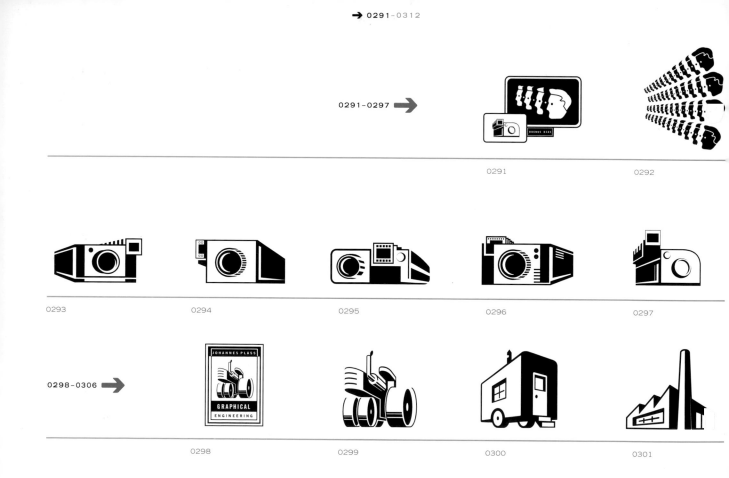

0291-0297 →

0291

0292

0293

0294

0295

0296

0297

0298-0306 →

0298

0299

0300

0301

0291–0297 Mutabor Online
0298–0301 Graphical Engineering

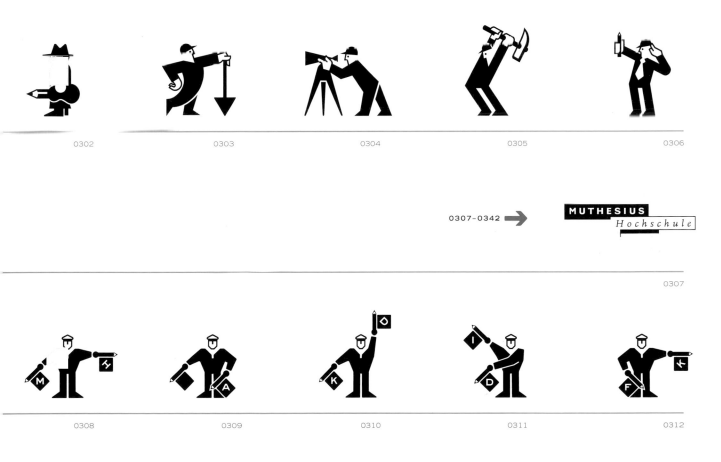

0302

0303

0304

0305

0306

0307-0342 ➡ **MUTHESIUS** *Hochschule*

0307

0308

0309

0310

0311

0312

0302–0306 Graphical Engineering
0307–0312 Muthesius Hochschule Kiel

0313

0314

0315

0316

0317

0318

0319

0320

0321

0322

0323

0324

0325

0326

0327

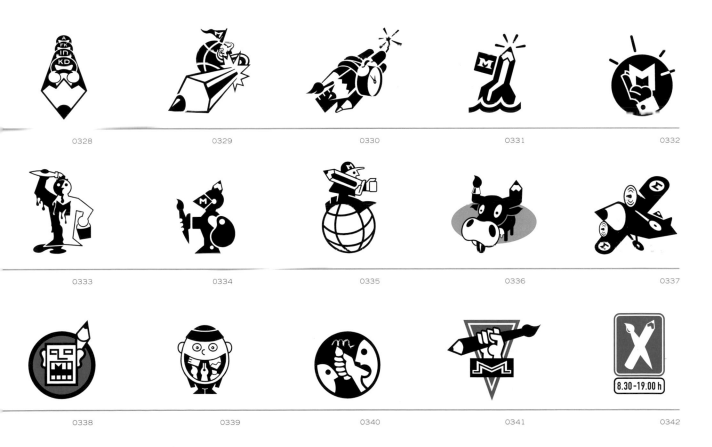

0328

0329

0330

0331

0332

0333

0334

0335

0336

0337

0338

0339

0340

0341

0342

0343-0424

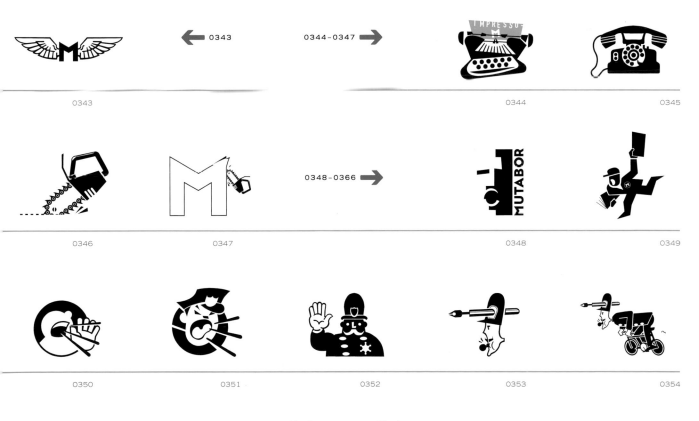

0343

0344–0347

0348–0366

0343

0344

0345

0346

0347

0348

0349

0350

0351

0352

0353

0354

0343 Mutabor 1 0344–0347 Mutabor 3
0348–0354 Mutabor 4

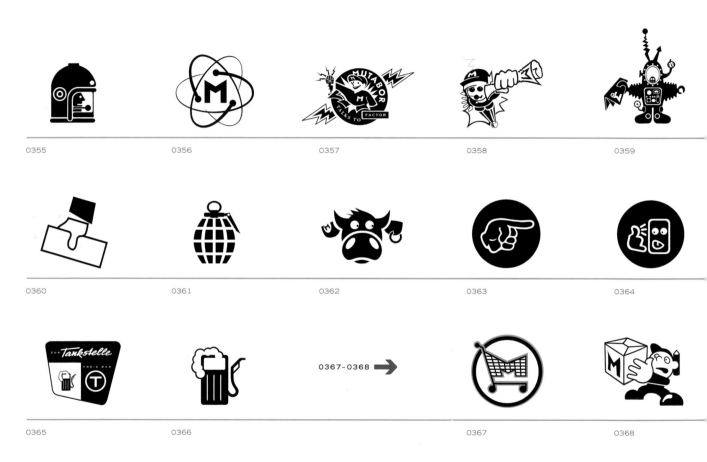

0355

0356

0357

0358

0359

0360

0361

0362

0363

0364

0365

0366

0367-0368 →

0367

0368

0355–0366 Mutabor 4
0367–0368 Mutabor 5

0369-0387 →

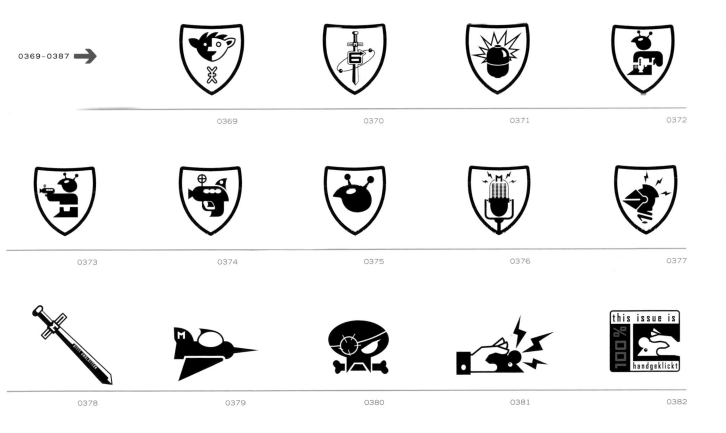

0369

0370

0371

0372

0373

0374

0375

0376

0377

0378

0379

0380

0381

0382

0388-0407 →

0383　0384　0385　0386　0387

0388　0389

0390　0391　0392　0393　0394

0383–0387 Mutabor 6
0388–0394 Mutabor 7

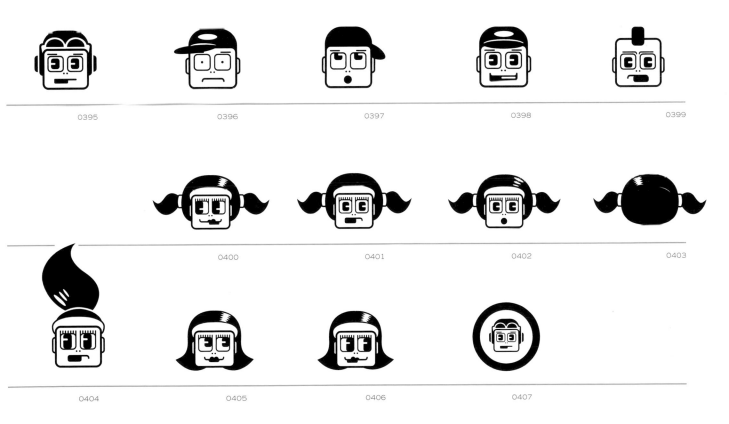

0395 0396 0397 0398 0399

0400 0401 0402 0403

0404 0405 0406 0407

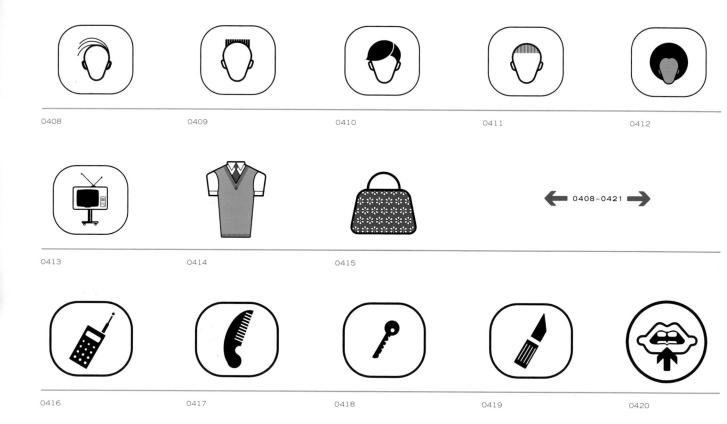

0408

0409

0410

0411

0412

0413

0414

0415

← 0408-0421 →

0416

0417

0418

0419

0420

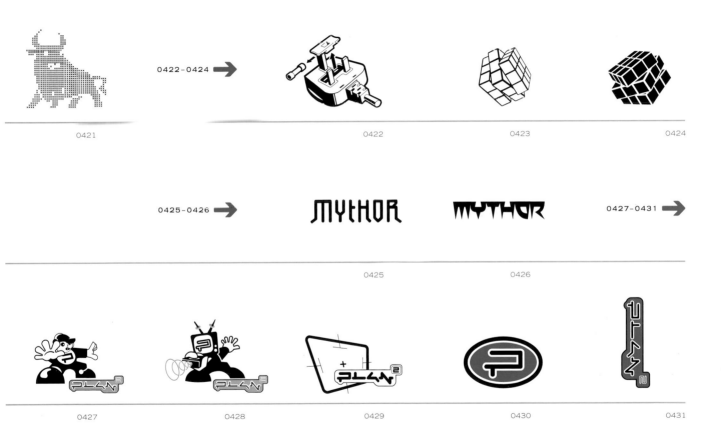

0421

0422-0424 →

0422

0423

0424

0425-0426 →

MYTHOR

MYTHOR

0427-0431 →

0425

0426

0427

0428

0429

0430

0431

0421 Mutabor 8 0422–0424 Mutabor 9
0425–0426 Mythor 0427–0431 Planquadrat

0432-0489 →

0432

0433

0434

0435

0436

0437

0438

0439

0440

0441

0442

0443

0444

0445

0446

0447

0448

0449

0450

0451

0452

0453

0454

0455

0456

0457

0458

0459

0460

0461

0462

0463

0464

0465

0466

0467

0468

0469

0470

0471

0472

0473

0474

0475

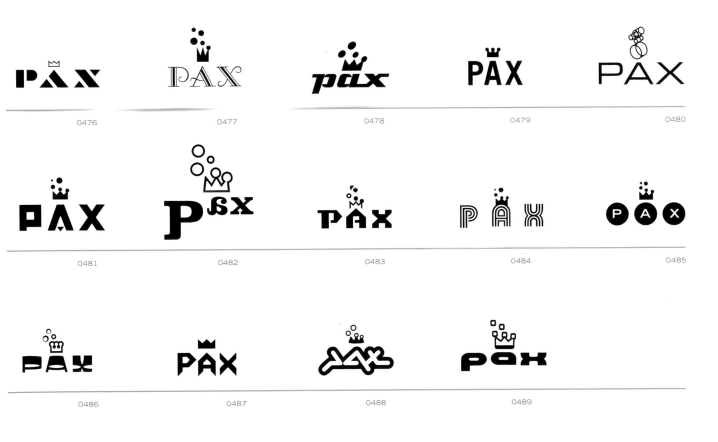

0476

0477

0478

0479

0480

0481

0482

0483

0484

0485

0486

0487

0488

0489

0490-0572

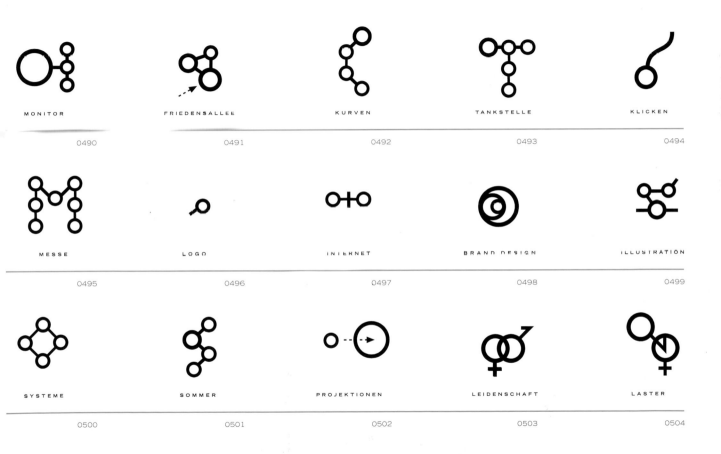

MONITOR

0490

FRIEDENSALLEE

0491

KURVEN

0492

TANKSTELLE

0493

KLICKEN

0494

MESSE

0495

LOGO

0496

INTERNET

0497

BRAND DESIGN

0498

ILLUSTRATION

0499

SYSTEME

0500

SOMMER

0501

PROJEKTIONEN

0502

LEIDENSCHAFT

0503

LASTER

0504

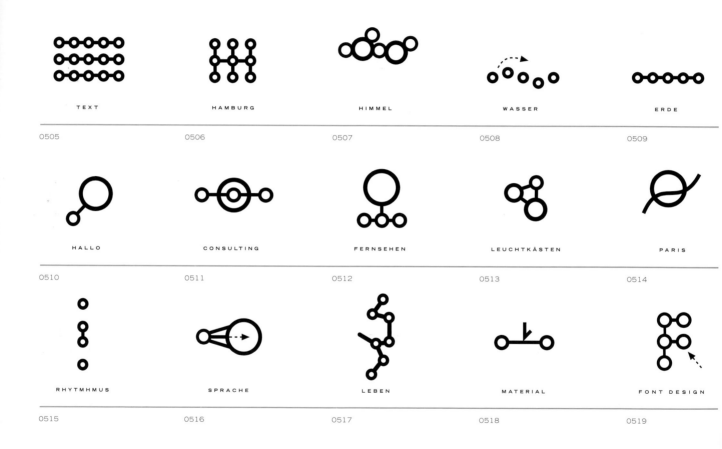

TEXT

0505

HAMBURG

0506

HIMMEL

0507

WASSER

0508

ERDE

0509

HALLO

0510

CONSULTING

0511

FERNSEHEN

0512

LEUCHTKÄSTEN

0513

PARIS

0514

RHYTMHMUS

0515

SPRACHE

0516

LEBEN

0517

MATERIAL

0518

FONT DESIGN

0519

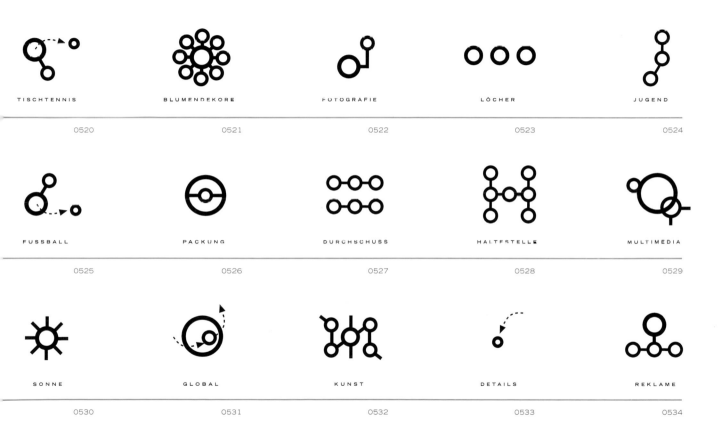

TISCHTENNIS

BLUMENDEKORE

FOTOGRAFIE

LÖCHER

JUGEND

0520

0521

0522

0523

0524

FUSSBALL

PACKUNG

DURCHSCHUSS

HALTESTELLE

MULTIMEDIA

0525

0526

0527

0528

0529

SONNE

GLOBAL

KUNST

DETAILS

REKLAME

0530

0531

0532

0533

0534

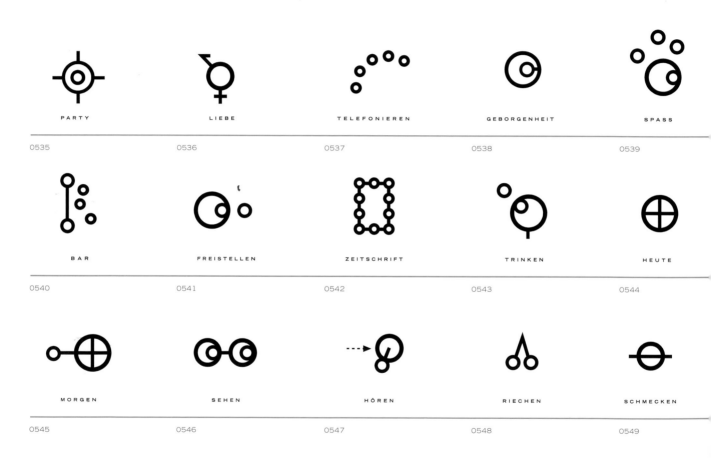

PARTY

LIEBE

TELEFONIEREN

GEBORGENHEIT

SPASS

0535

0536

0537

0538

0539

BAR

FREISTELLEN

ZEITSCHRIFT

TRINKEN

HEUTE

0540

0541

0542

0543

0544

MORGEN

SEHEN

HÖREN

RIECHEN

SCHMECKEN

0545

0546

0547

0548

0549

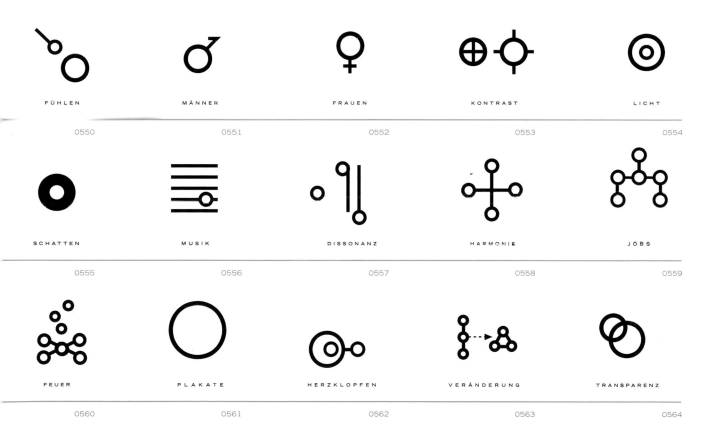

FÜHLEN	MÄNNER	FRAUEN	KONTRAST	LICHT
0550	0551	0552	0553	0554
SCHATTEN	MUSIK	DISSONANZ	HARMONIE	JÖBS
0555	0556	0557	0558	0559
FEUER	PLAKATE	HERZKLOPFEN	VERÄNDERUNG	TRANSPARENZ
0560	0561	0562	0563	0564

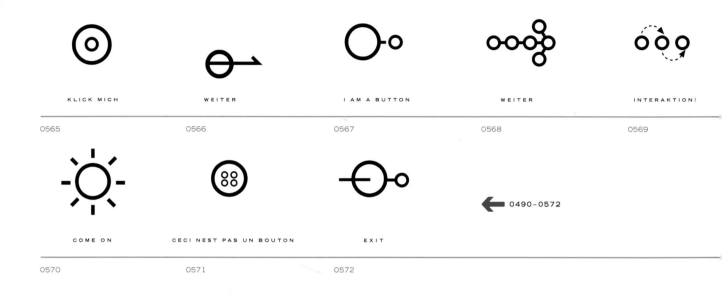

KLICK MICH   WEITER   I AM A BUTTON   WEITER   INTERAKTION!

0565   0566   0567   0568   0569

COME ON   CECI NEST PAS UN BOUTON   EXIT   ← 0490-0572

0570   0571   0572

0573-0755

0573

0574

0575

0576

0577

0578

0579

0580

0581

0582

0583

0584

0585

0586

← 0573-0586

0587-0600 ➡

0587

0588

0589

0590

0591

0592

0593

0594

0595

0596

0597

0598

0599

0600

0601-0642 →

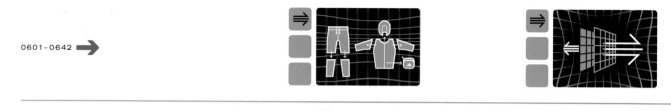

0601

0602

chamoix

reflective

uv protection

0603

0604

0605

upf 50

cardio bra

care instructions

0606

0607

0608

performance cut

stow away

waterproof

0609 0610 0611

performa fresh

microfibre

0612 0613 0614

breathable

reversible

real down

0615 0616 0617

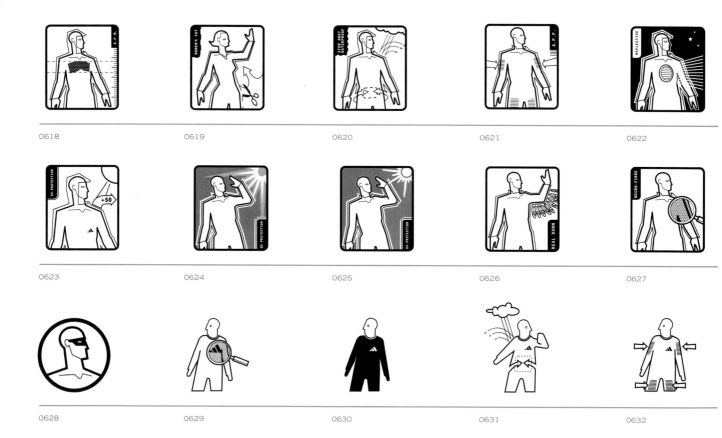

0618

0619

0620

0621

0622

0623

0624

0625

0626

0627

0628

0629

0630

0631

0632

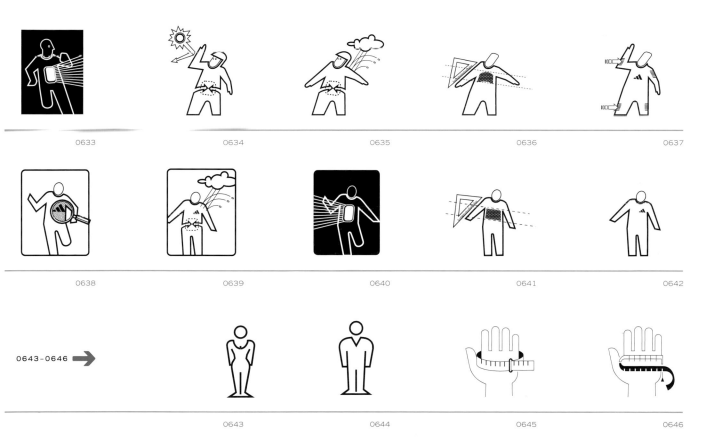

0633

0634

0635

0636

0637

0638

0639

0640

0641

0642

0643-0646

0643

0644

0645

0646

0633–0642 Adidas
0643–0646 Adidas Packaging

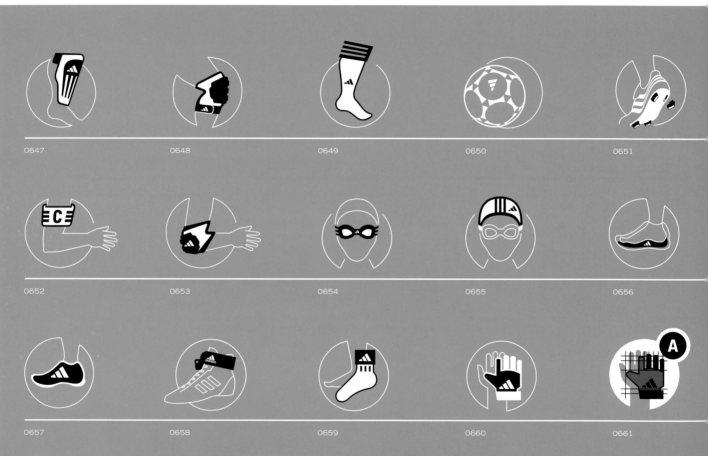

0647

0648

0649

0650

0651

0652

0653

0654

0655

0656

0657

0658

0659

0660

0661

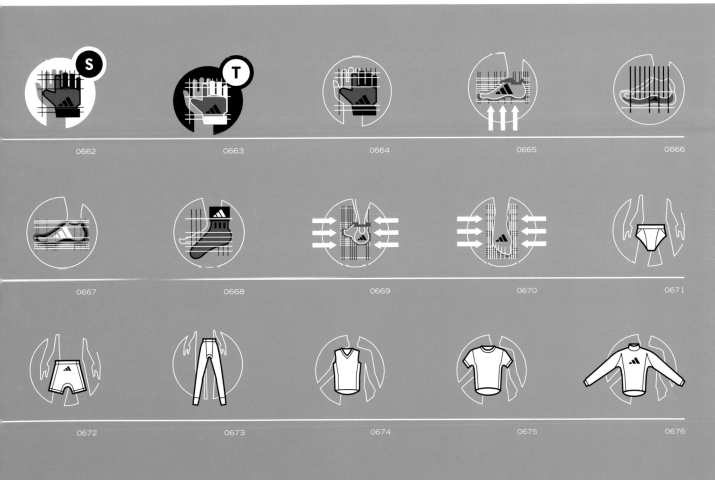

0662

0663

0664

0665

0666

0667

0668

0669

0670

0671

0672

0673

0674

0675

0676

0662—0676 Adidas Packaging

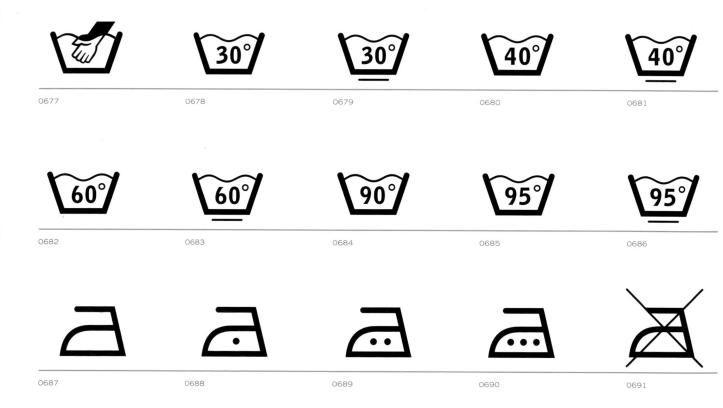

0677

0678

0679

0680

0681

0682

0683

0684

0685

0686

0687

0688

0689

0690

0691

0677–0691 Adidas Dingbats

0692	0693	0694	0695	0696
0697	0698	0699	0700	0701
0702	0703	0704	0705	0706

0692–0706 Adidas Dingbats

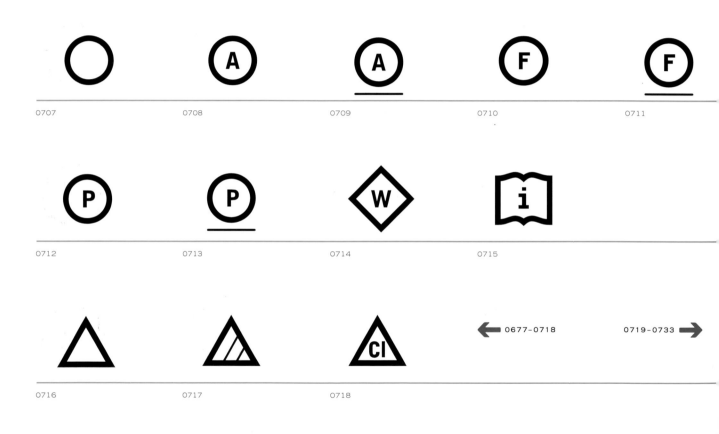

0707

0708

0709

0710

0711

0712

0713

0714

0715

0716

0717

0718

← 0677-0718

0719-0733 →

0707–0718 Adidas Dingbats

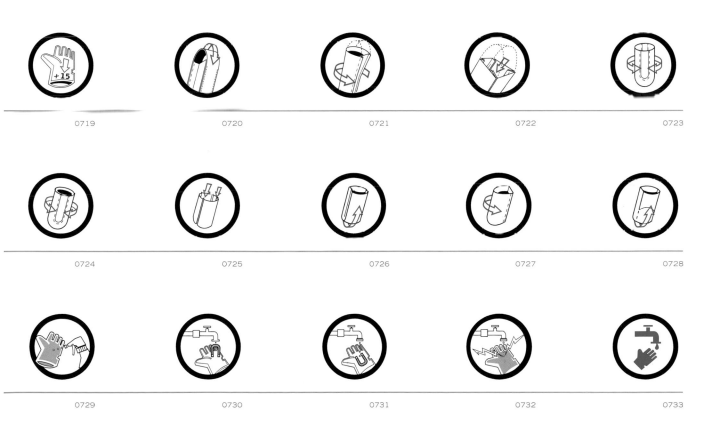

0719   0720   0721   0722   0723

0724   0725   0726   0727   0728

0729   0730   0731   0732   0733

0719–0733 Adidas Packaging

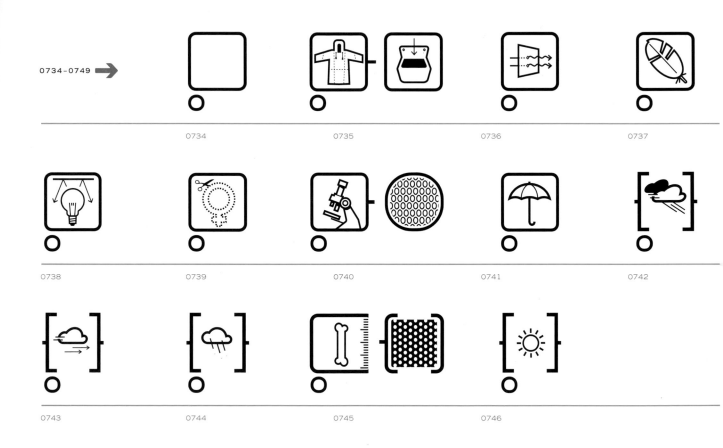

0734-0749 ➡

0734

0735

0736

0737

0738

0739

0740

0741

0742

0743

0744

0745

0746

0747

0748

0749

0750 0755 ➡

0750

0751

0752

0753

0754

0755

0747–0749 Adidas
0750–0755 Adidas Equipment

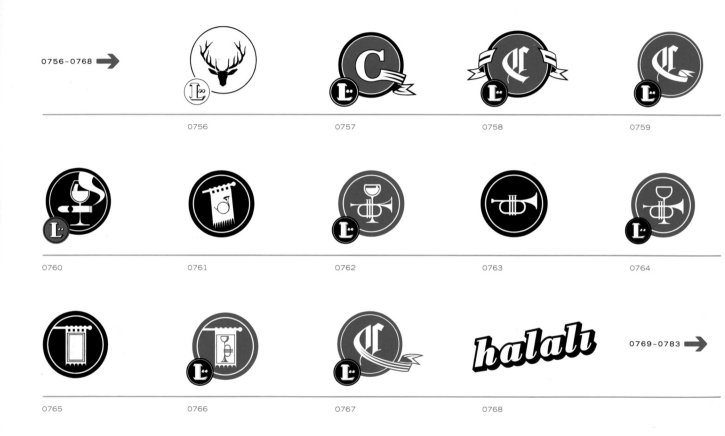

0756-0768 →

0756

0757

0758

0759

0760

0761

0762

0763

0764

0765

0766

0767

0768

0769-0783 →

0769

0770

0771

0772

0773

0774

0775

0776

0777

0778

0779

0780

0781

0782

0783

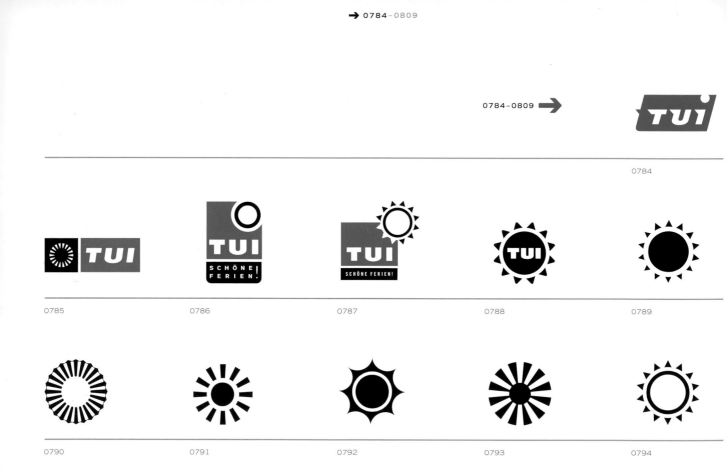

0784–0809 →

0784

0785 0786 0787 0788 0789

0790 0791 0792 0793 0794

0795

0796

0797

0798

0799

0800

0801

0802

0803

0804

0805

0806

0807

0808

0809

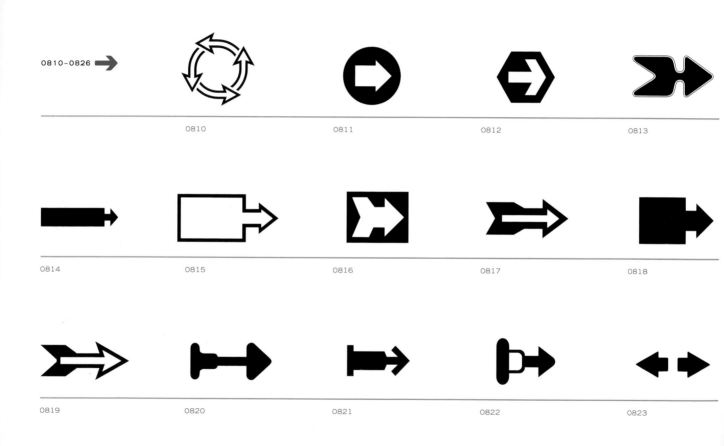

0810-0826

0810

0811

0812

0813

0814

0815

0816

0817

0818

0819

0820

0821

0822

0823

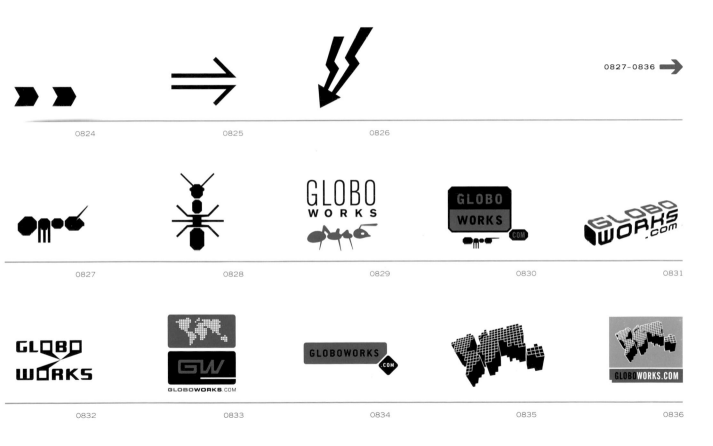

0827-0836

0824

0825

0826

0827

0828

0829

0830

0831

0832

0833

0834

0835

0836

0824–0826 Pfeile
0827–0836 Globo Works

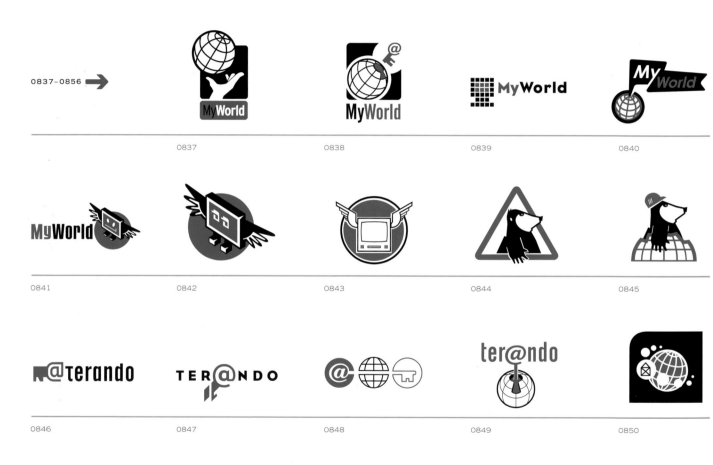

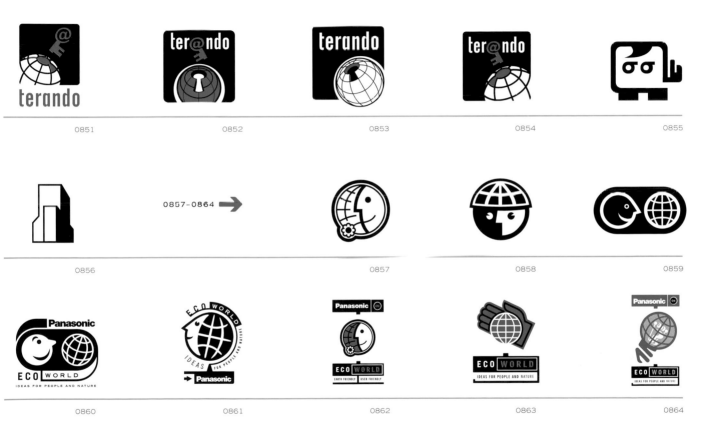

0851 0852 0853 0854 0855

0856 0857-0864 ➔ 0857 0858 0859

0860 0861 0862 0863 0864

0851–0856 MyWorld / Terando
0857–0864 Panasonic Eco World

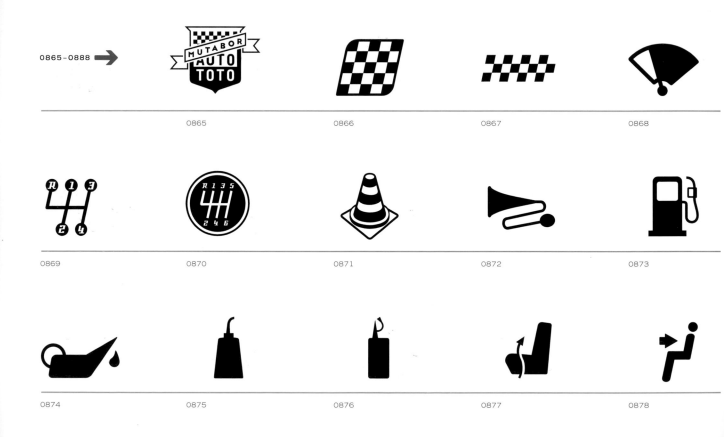

0865–0888 →

0865

0866

0867

0868

0869

0870

0871

0872

0873

0874

0875

0876

0877

0878

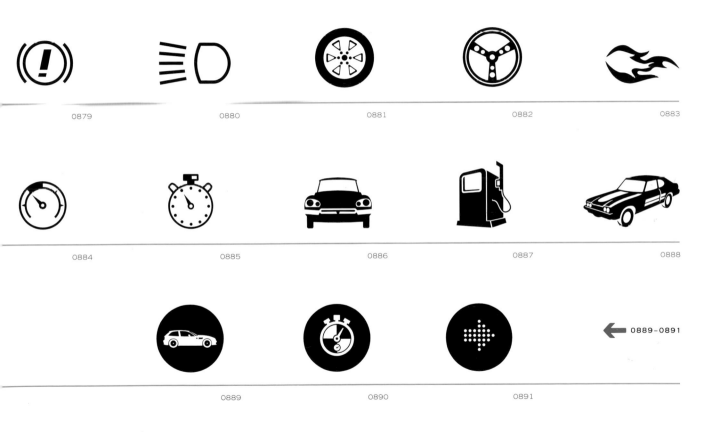

0879

0880

0881

0882

0883

0884

0885

0886

0887

0888

0889

0890

0891

0889–0891

0879–0888 Turbo Dingbats
0889–0891 M-Coupe

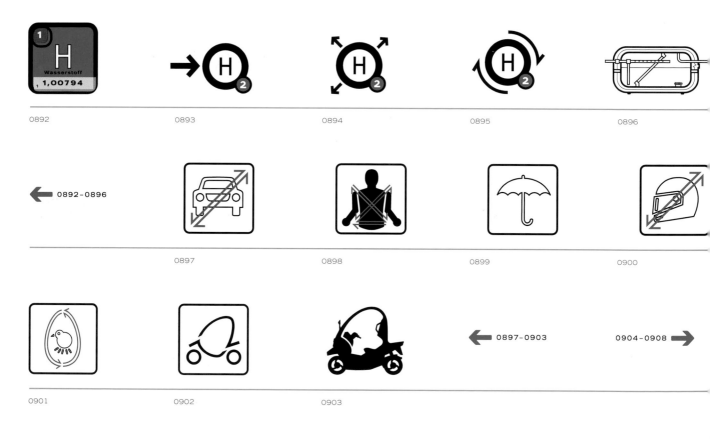

0892

0893

0894

0895

0896

← 0892-0896

0897

0898

0899

0900

0901

0902

0903

← 0897-0903

0904-0908 →

0892–0896 BMW H2
0897–0903 BMW C1

0904

BEWEGUNG MOTION

0905

0906

FAHRWERK

0907

VELOX

0908

0900 →

0909

0910–0915 →

0910

0911

0912

0913

0914

0915

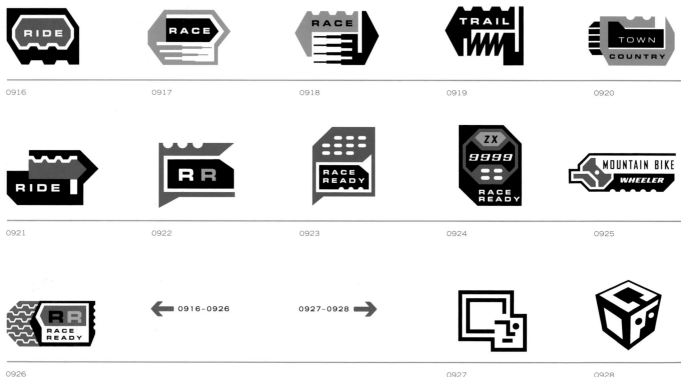

0916

0917

0918

0919

0920

0921

0922

0923

0924

0925

0926

← 0916-0926

0927-0928 →

0927

0928

0916–0926 Wheeler
0927–0928 Thin Client Forum

0929

0930

0931

0932

0929–0932

0933–0935

0933

0934

0935

0936–0940

0936

0937

0938

0939

0940

0929–0932 Inline 0933–0935 Soft Werft
0936–0940 Nastrovje Potsdam

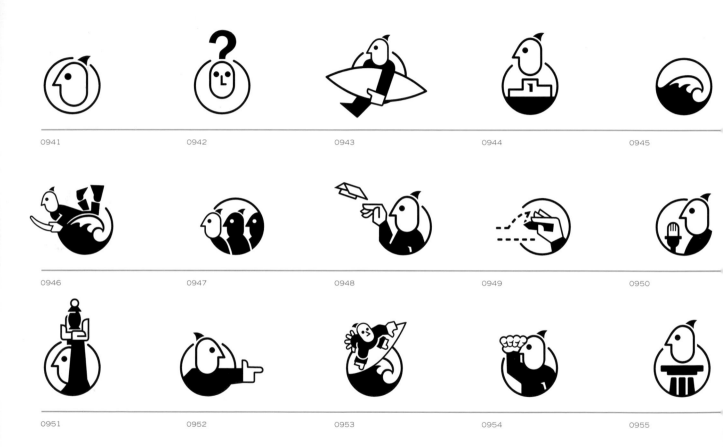

0941

0942

0943

0944

0945

0946

0947

0948

0949

0950

0951

0952

0953

0954

0955

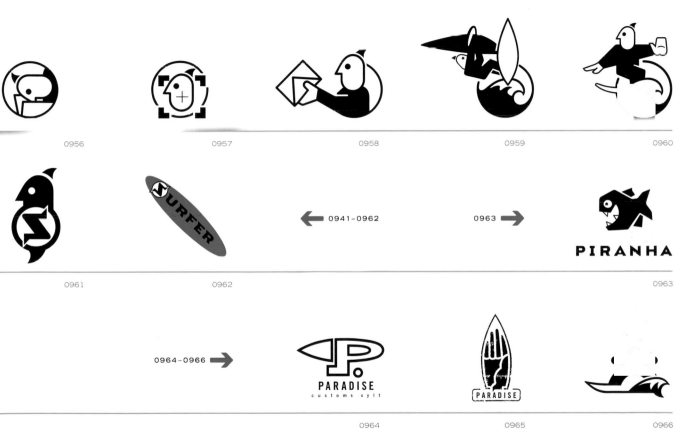

0956

0957

0958

0959

0960

0961

0962

← 0941–0962

0963 →

PIRANHA

0963

0964–0966 →

PARADISE
customs sylt

PARADISE

0964

0965

0966

0956–0962 Surfers Magazine 0963 Piranha
0964–0966 Paradise

0967–0985 →

0967

0968

0969

0970

0971

0972

0973

0974

0975

0976

0977

0978

0979

0980

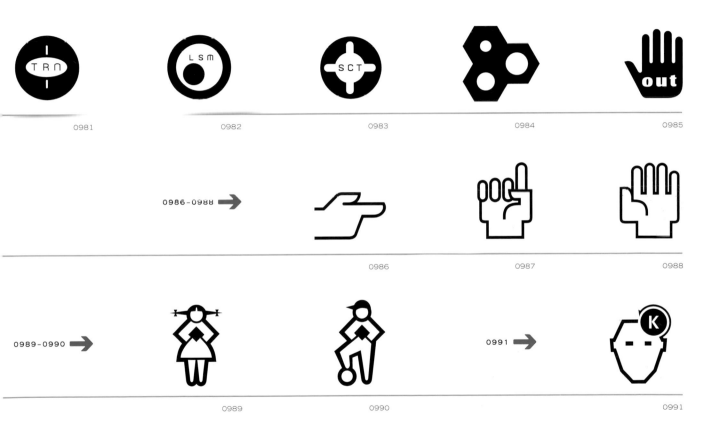

0981

0982

0983

0984

0985

0986–0988 ➔

0986

0987

0988

0989–0990 ➔

0989

0990

0991 ➔

0991

0981–0985 Rotring Core 0986–0988 Football
0989–0990 HSV 0991 Debis

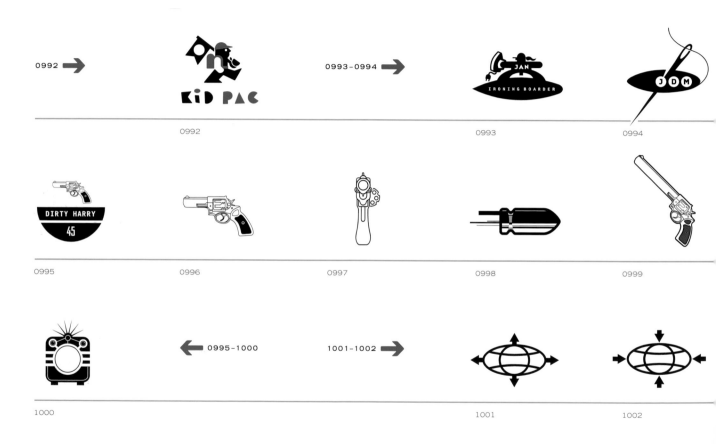

0992 →

KiD PAC

0992

0993–0994 →

0993

0994

DIRTY HARRY
45

0995

0996

0997

0998

0999

1000

← 0995–1000

1001–1002 →

1001

1002

0992 Kid Pac **0993–0994** Jan Derek Müller
0995–1000 Universal Dirty Harry **1001–1002** Walter Karger

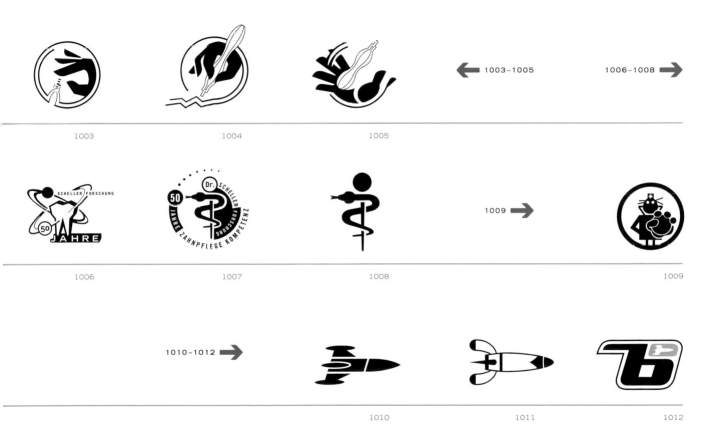

1003   1004   1005

← 1003–1005   1006–1008 →

1006   1007   1008   1009 →

1009

1010–1012 →

1010   1011   1012

1003–1005 Stabilo **1006–1008** Dr. Scheller
1009 Praxis Dr. Thiel **1010–1012** Berry Künzel

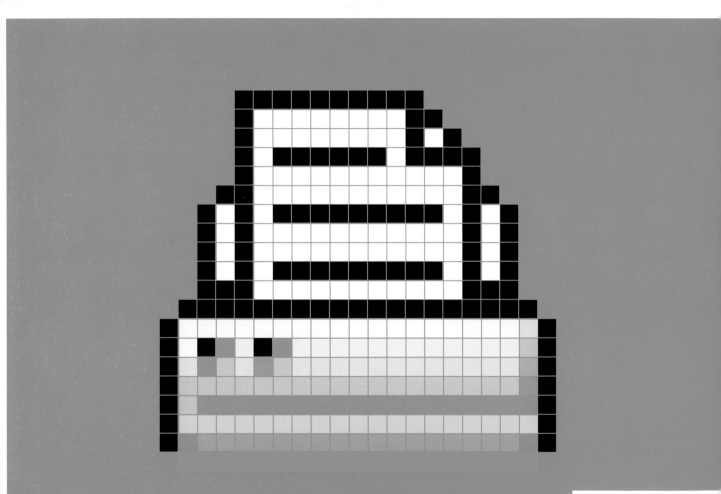

1013-1056

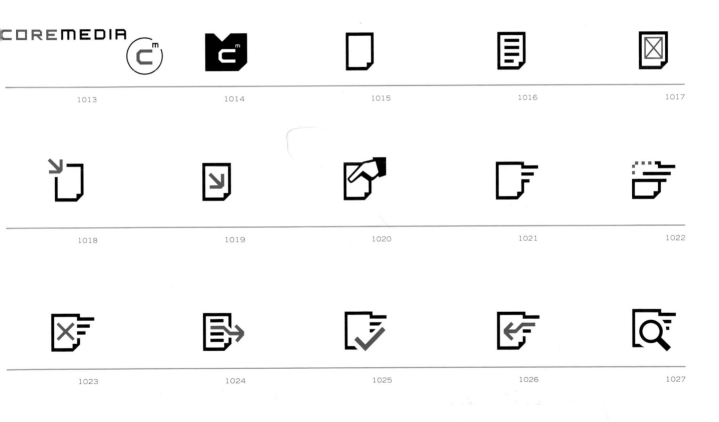

1013	1014	1015	1016	1017
1018	1019	1020	1021	1022
1023	1024	1025	1026	1027

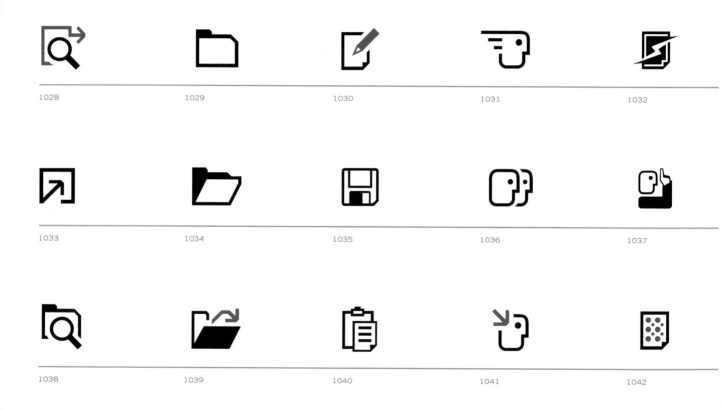

1028

1029

1030

1031

1032

1033

1034

1035

1036

1037

1038

1039

1040

1041

1042

1043	1044	1045	1046	1047

1048	1049	1050	1051	1052

1053	1054	1055	1056

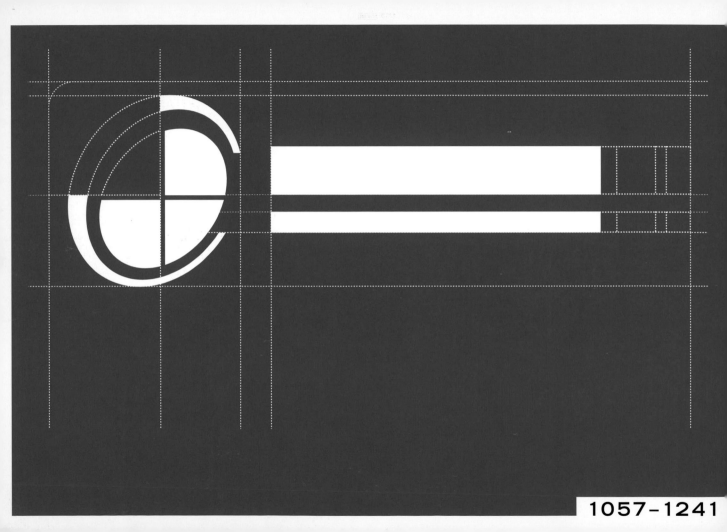

1057-1241

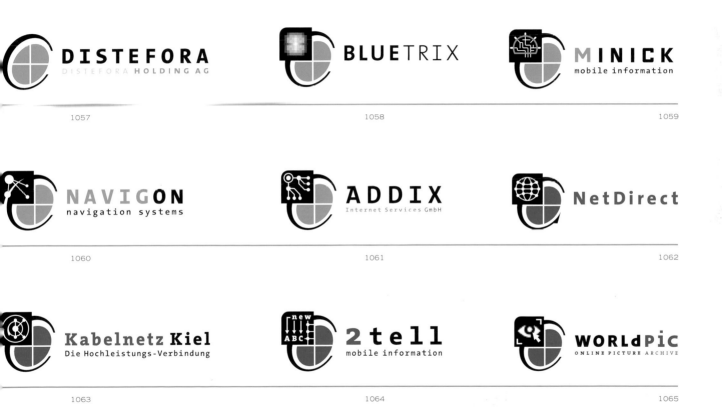

DISTEFORA
DISTEFORA HOLDING AG

1057

BLUETRIX

1058

M INICK
mobile information

1059

NAVIGON
navigation systems

1060

ADDIX
Internet Services GmbH

1061

NetDirect

1062

Kabelnetz Kiel
Die Hochleistungs-Verbindung

1063

2tell
mobile information

1064

WORLdPiC
ONLINE PICTURE ARCHIVE

1065

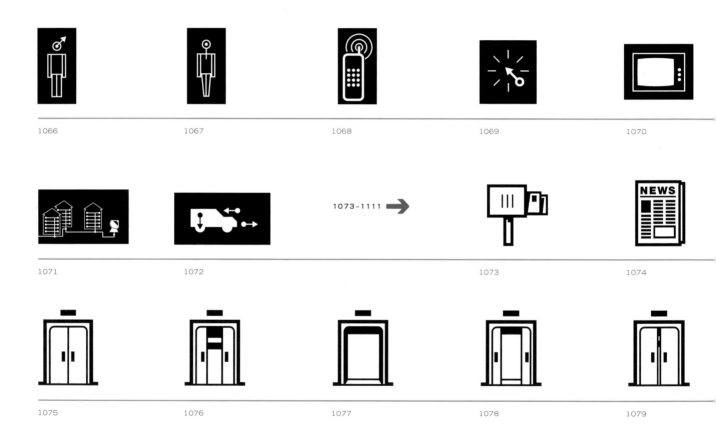

1066   1067   1068   1069   1070

1071   1072   1073-1111 →   1073   1074

1075   1076   1077   1078   1079

1066–1072 Distefora
1073–1079 Ision

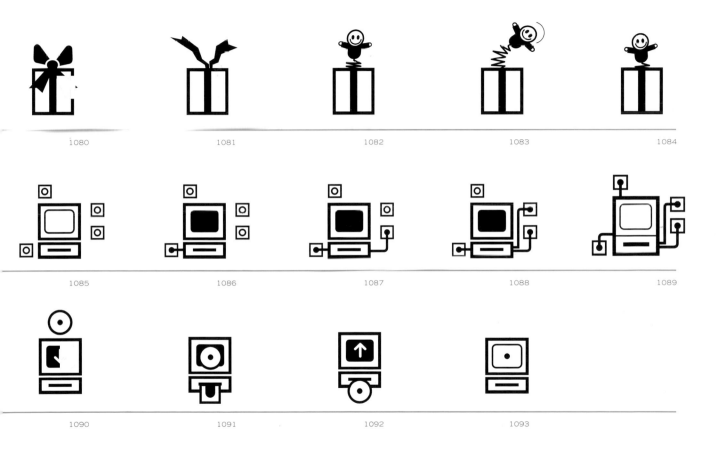

1080

1081

1082

1083

1084

1085

1086

1087

1088

1089

1090

1091

1092

1093

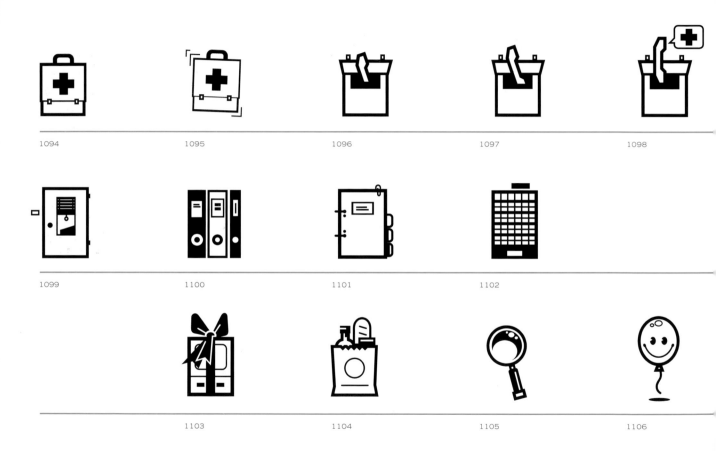

1094

1095

1096

1097

1098

1099

1100

1101

1102

1103

1104

1105

1106

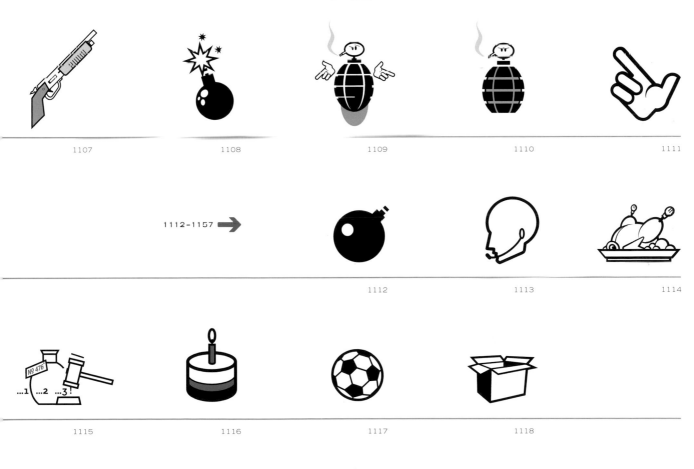

1107

1108

1109

1110

1111

1112–1157 ➡

1112

1113

1114

1115

1116

1117

1118

1107–1111 Ision
1112–1118 Minick

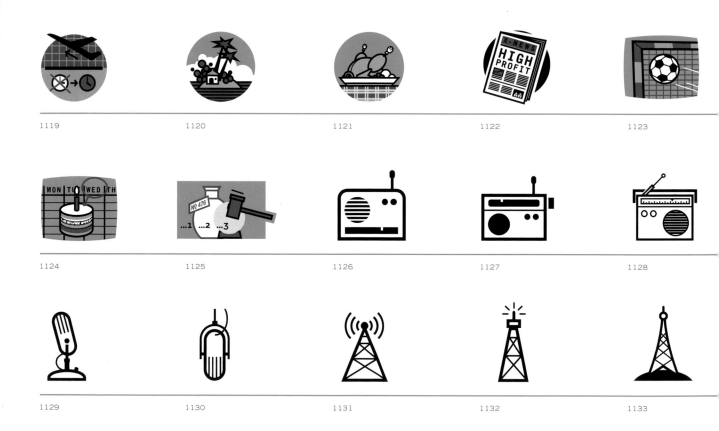

1119

1120

1121

1122

1123

1124

1125

1126

1127

1128

1129

1130

1131

1132

1133

1134   1135   1136   1137   1138

1139   1140   1141   1142

1143   1144   1145   1146   1147

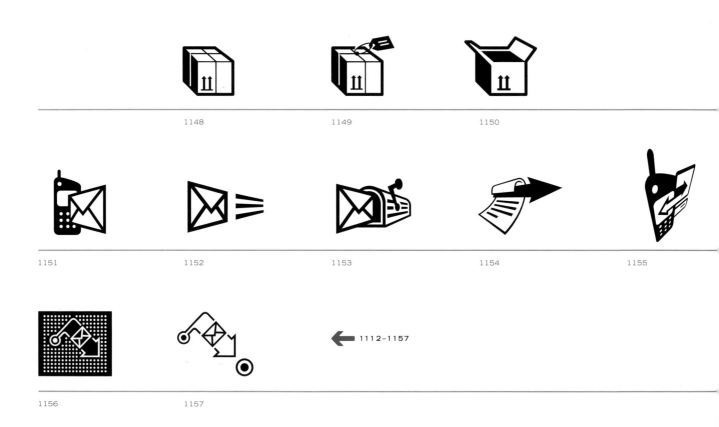

1148

1149

1150

1151

1152

1153

1154

1155

← 1112–1157

1156

1157

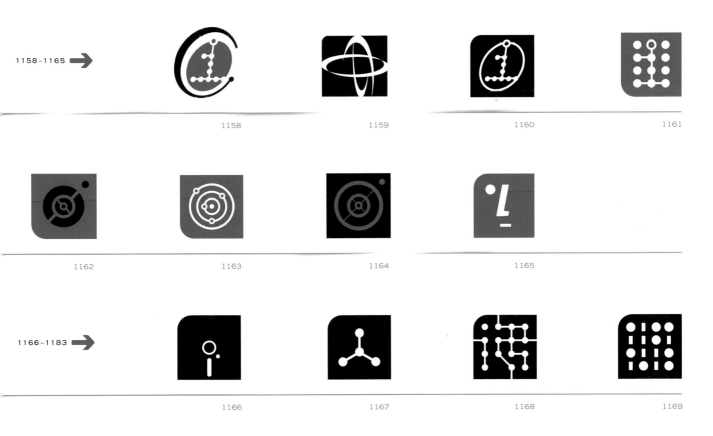

1158–1165 →

1158

1159

1160

1161

1162

1163

1164

1165

1166–1183 →

1166

1167

1168

1169

1158–1165 Ision
1166–1169 Distefora

1170

1171

1172

1173

1174

1175

1176

1177

1178

1179

1180

1181

1182

1183

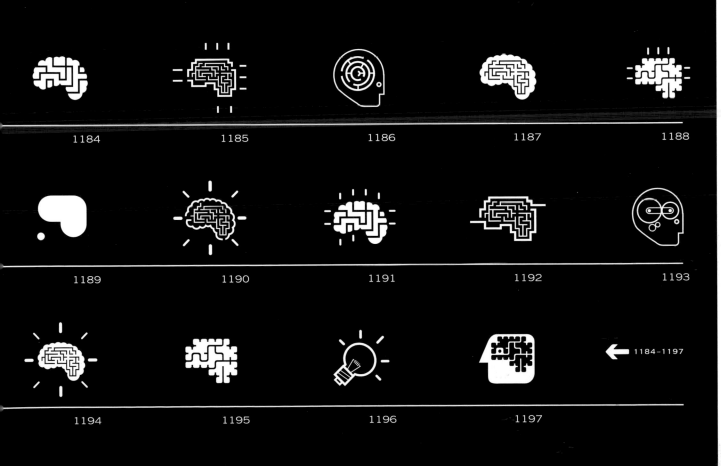

1184

1185

1186

1187

1188

1189

1190

1191

1192

1193

1194

1195

1196

1197

1184–1197

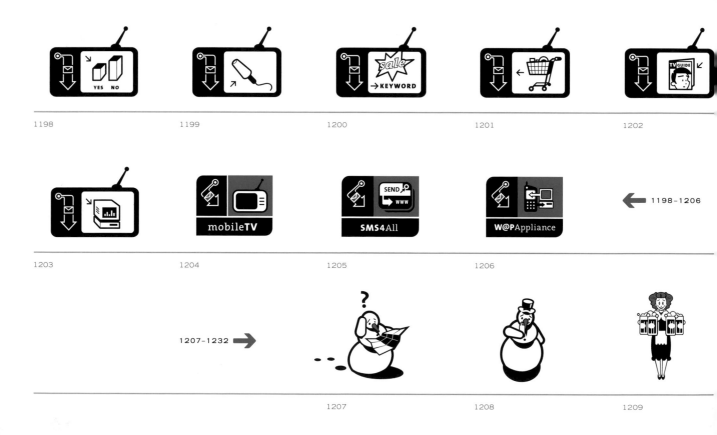

1198   1199   1200   1201   1202

1203   1204   1205   1206   ← 1198-1206

1207-1232 →

1207   1208   1209

1198–1206 Minick
1207–1209 Distefora

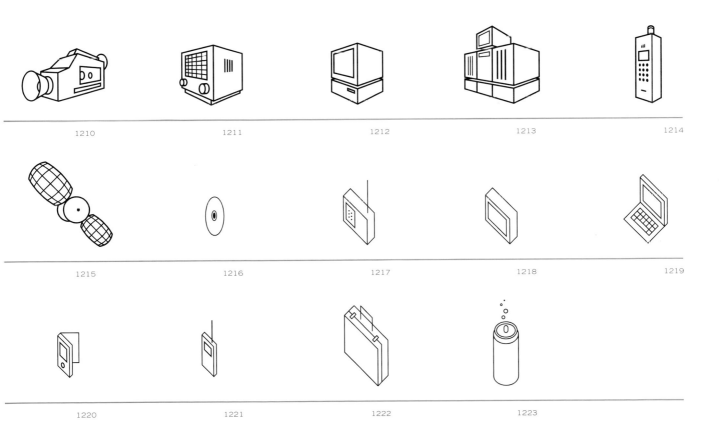

1210

1211

1212

1213

1214

1215

1216

1217

1218

1219

1220

1221

1222

1223

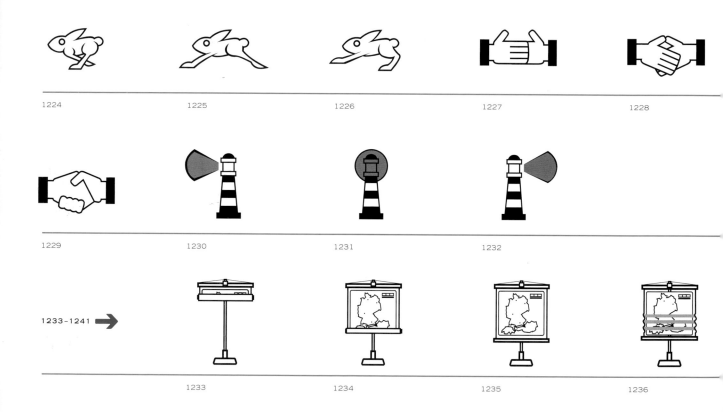

1224

1225

1226

1227

1228

1229

1230

1231

1232

1233-1241 ➜

1233

1234

1235

1236

1224–1232 Distefora
1233–1236 IS Internet Services

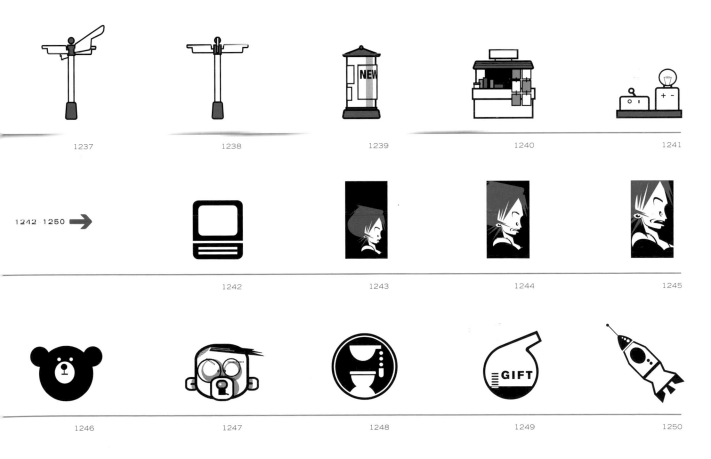

1237

1238

1239

1240

1241

1242 – 1250 →

1242

1243

1244

1245

1246

1247

1248

1249

1250

NEW

GIFT

1237–1241 IS Internet Services
1242–1250 Studien

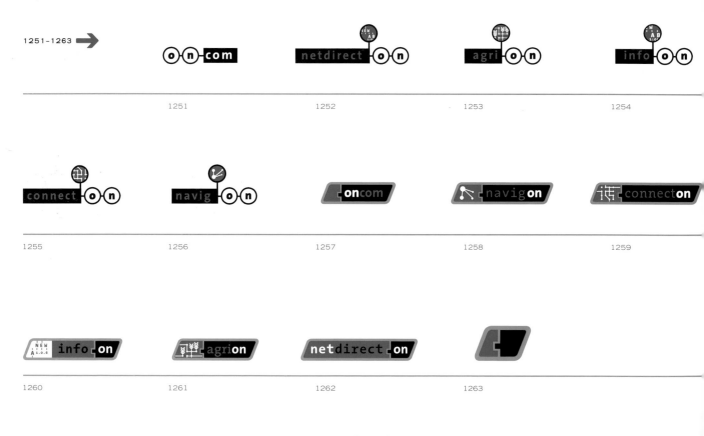

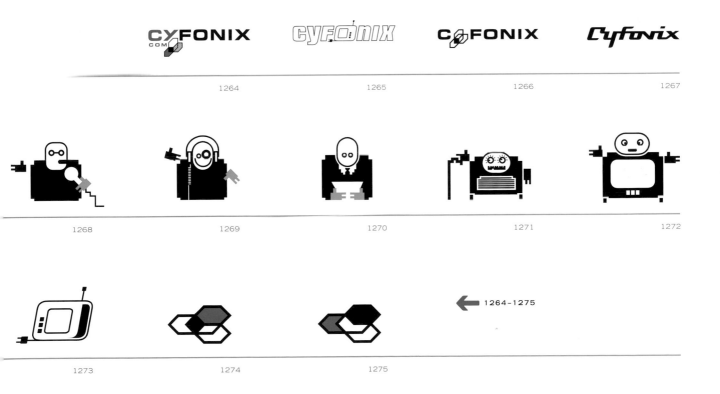

1264 1265 1266 1267 1268 1269 1270 1271 1272 1273 1274 1275

1264–1275

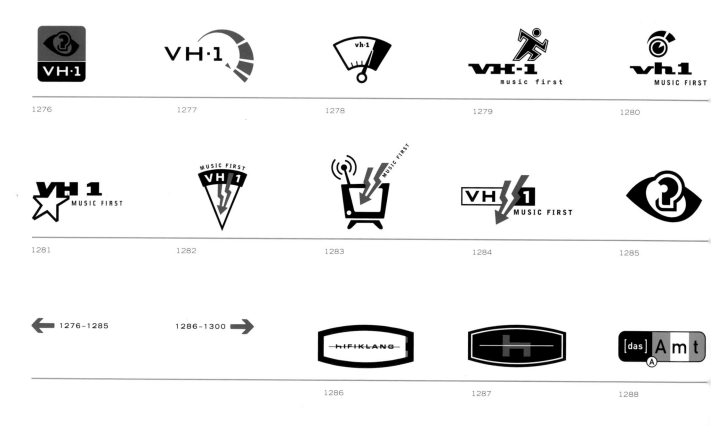

1276

1277

1278

1279

1280

1281

1282

1283

1284

1285

← 1276-1285   1286-1300 →

1286

1287

1288

1276–1285 VH-1
1286–1288 Studien

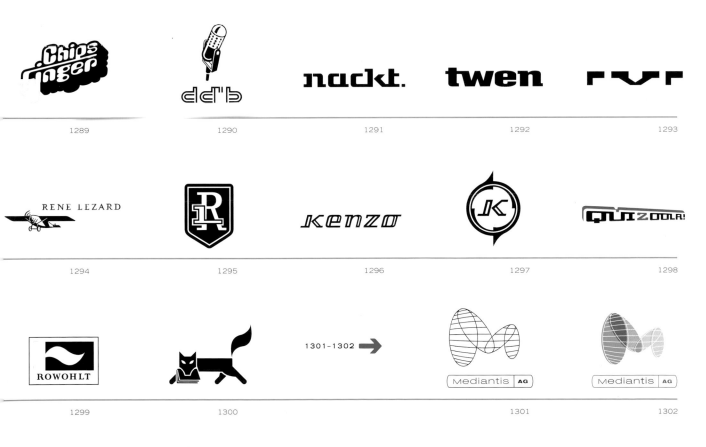

1289

1290

1291

1292

1293

1294

1295

1296

1297

1298

1299

1300

1301–1302

1301

1302

1289–1300 Studien
1301–1302 Mediantis

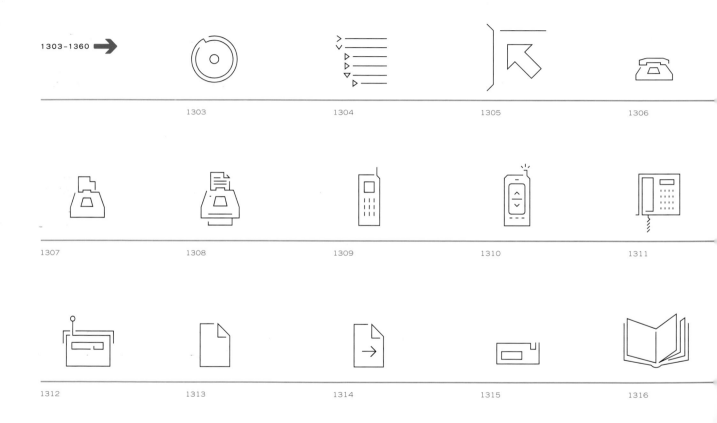

1303-1360 →

1303

1304

1305

1306

1307

1308

1309

1310

1311

1312

1313

1314

1315

1316

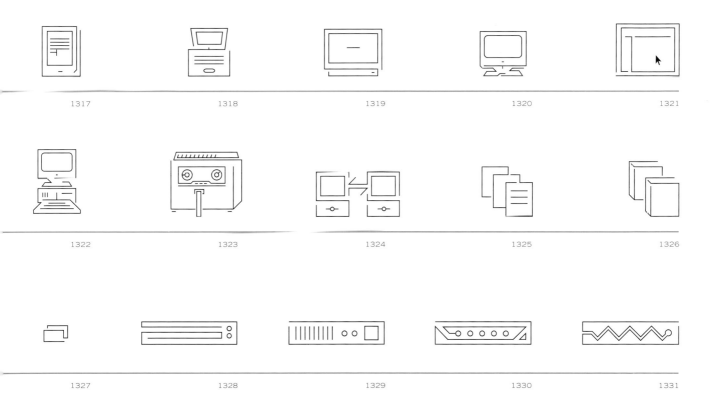

1317

1318

1319

1320

1321

1322

1323

1324

1325

1326

1327

1328

1329

1330

1331

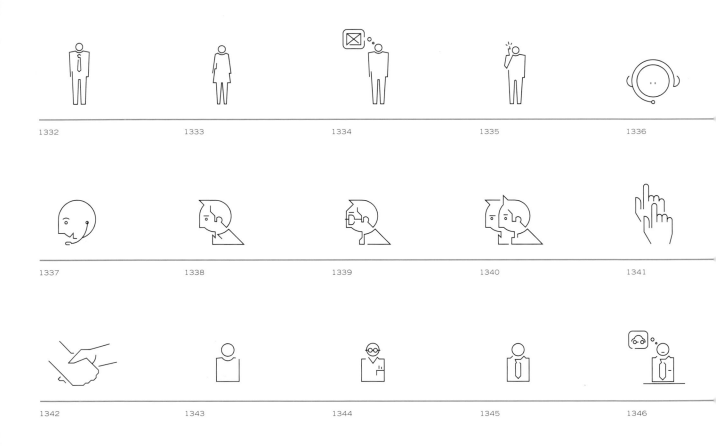

1332

1333

1334

1335

1336

1337

1338

1339

1340

1341

1342

1343

1344

1345

1346

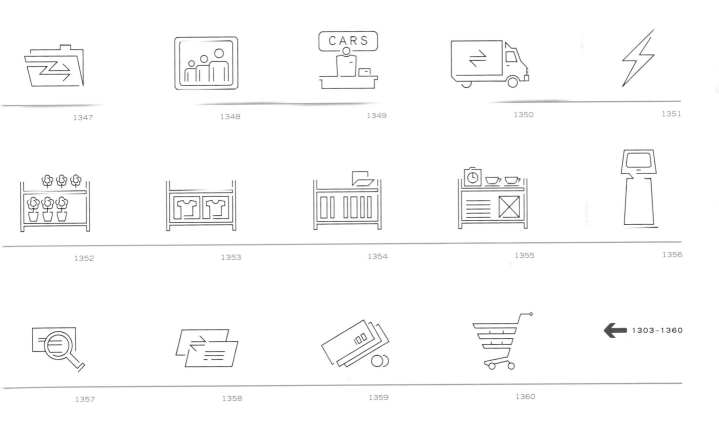

1347

1348

1349

1350

1351

1352

1353

1354

1355

1356

1357

1358

1359

1360

1303–1360

Index  ALL OF THE ICONS FROM A TO Z

➜ (Pages 188/189. Icon selection and classification...)

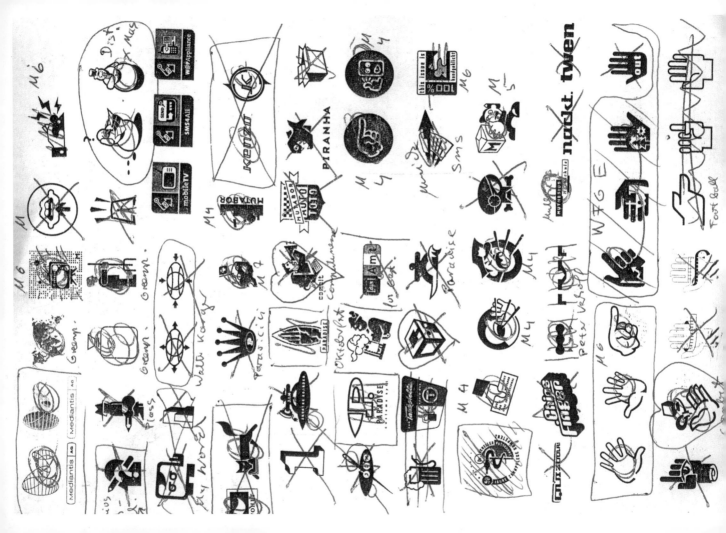

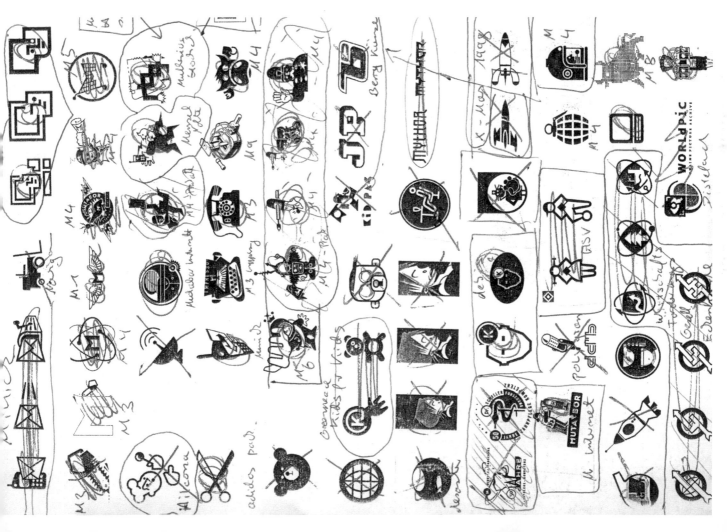

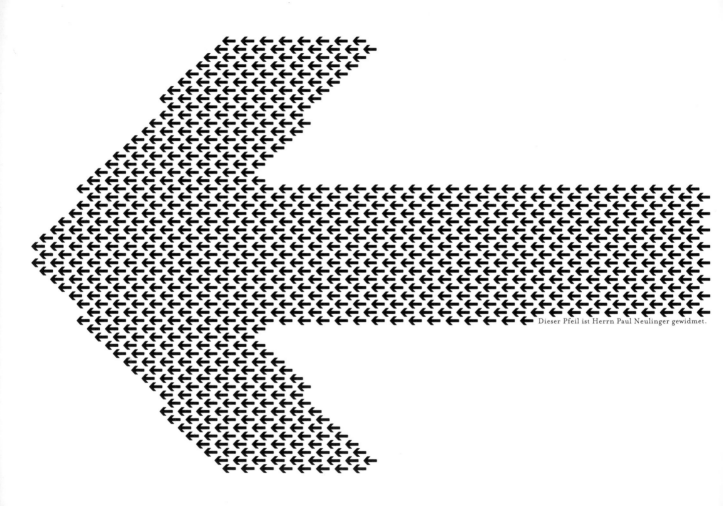

Dieser Pfeil ist Herrn Paul Neulinger gewidmet.

←

Please notice the direction of reading; start your studies on page OOI

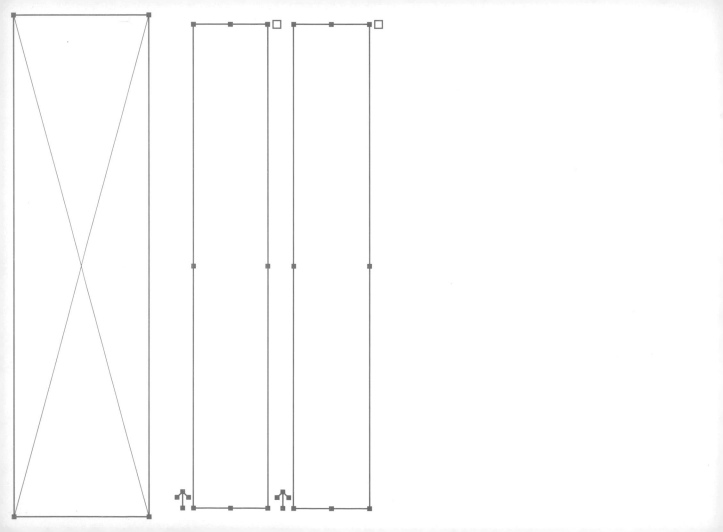